RESILIENCE

Your Superpower

for Authentic Leadership
(and Life)

Colette
To your
great leadership
Cynthia

TABLE OF CONTENTS

The Book: What Is in It for You

Why fit in when you were born to stand out?
—Dr. Seuss

More and more people today are distracted. Work-life balance is a challenge. Stressors at work don't seem to have an end to them, and many feel powerless to change any of it. People go to work on autopilot just to get through the day; seventy percent of the workforce is disengaged from their jobs. This includes managers. There is a problem in healthcare that is not being solved.

There is an epidemic of disillusionment. Professionals at all levels are struggling with disappointment, anger, resentment, and powerlessness because of the gap between what they thought they would be doing and what they are actually doing. There is less and less perceived value in the effort professionals are giving to their jobs. The potential for great talent, innovation, and creativity exists in scores of professionals who continue to show up for work, shut down, not knowing what else to do.

There is something sacred about working in healthcare. Whether you are on the frontlines caring for patients or the leader—all the way to the administration—it is an honor to be with people at birth, death, in sickness and health. We all will experience vulnerability along this continuum of life, and as healthcare professional, it is our job and responsibility to make it a dignified experience. Technology, pharmacology, and all the other great advances that have saved and extended lives can only happen because of the professionals who give of themselves every day to make a difference. It is our responsibility to also dignify the experience of the professionals and leaders who sacrifice themselves in the process.

This book offers my solution that will bridge that gap and restore meaning to your life—on and off the job. William James, called one of the most influential philosopher of all time, wrote, "The great problem of life seems to be how to keep body and soul together." This dilemma motivated this book.

The reality check is this: regardless of what is happening on the job, it is what you tell yourself about what is happening that creates the barrier to a better quality of life. Your inner game is what will allow you to access your fullest potential. This is the superpower of resilience.

If you have been caught up in an endless "to-do" list and lost touch with the meaning behind what you are doing, you may be ignoring the very choices you need to make that will support a fulfilled and quality life. Exercise, healthy diet, prayer, meditation, and good sleep get compromised to get "one more thing" done. At the end of the day, after putting out fires and dodging bullets, it isn't any wonder there is a lack of satisfaction. The focus on what is more urgent keeps you from what is most important.

Are you ready to learn a new way "to do" work?

With technology taking over more and more of daily life, distraction becomes the new normal. With distraction comes the emotional hijacking from the flight or fight reaction. The cycle is set up with reactive emotions, and wasted energy and conflict becomes normal. Opportunity for solutions is lost in the struggle. The stress reaction is a primitive survival reaction, and when triggered, everything is experienced as a threat. There doesn't seem to be enough of anything, especially time and attention. Attention is lost in the tunnel vision typical in the stress reaction. This book introduces you to a system of energy management so you can consistently perform at a higher level without draining yourself in the process. It will help you be more efficient and creative and enjoy your life more.

This book is written to help you master your attention by activating the superpower of resilience. When you are distracted by overwhelm and caught up in your own stress reaction, you lose the ability to focus. When you are going from one urgent crisis to the next, you will miss nuances in conversations, not take the time to actively listen, and short-change the very people who are key to your success. You miss the impact stress is having on you and the impact you are having on others. Relationships falter, and the crisis mode becomes normal. This is the road to burnout.

How to Get the Most Out of This Book

As you read, you will have insights to help you shift your perspective. If you answer the questions and reflect on your answers, you will change your thinking. This will lead to better choices in your day. Share this book, purchase a copy for every member of your team (bulk discounts are available), and make it part of a book study for the quarter. Keep a notebook in your department and have people write out their insights and ideas that come up for them as you all learn to reflect and take ownership of the solution.

Recognize that you have untapped potential that is being squelched because of a lack of focus. Shift from needing to manage time to managing your energy. Time is a finite resource. The nature of energy is that it is unlimited. You are pure energy, and as you understand the principles in this book, you will learn to get more accomplished with less effort. The old adage *time is money* changes to *energy is money*. This shift in thinking immediately creates an abundant mindset. You have the resources you need inside of you, and this book will introduce you to the tools to experience that abundance along with your brilliance.

This book is part of the Resilient Leader System, a program for high-performance leadership (and life). This system teaches you to access the dimensions of emotional intelligence and introduces powerful strategies to quickly unhook you from the stress reaction so you can perform at your best. I provide one-on-one coaching, a combination of online programs, live retreats, and an ongoing Mastermind program. This program can be conducted in your organization as part of your professional development. If you are responsible for setting up professional development, contact me and let's discuss options and ideas to help you best satisfy your goals. If you would like to discuss how this program might benefit you, contact me and let's schedule a complimentary Power-Up Session; details are in the back of the book.

This book starts out with some shocking numbers on turnover and toxicity in healthcare. I want you to see the compelling argument for taking immediate action to change your relationship with work. Then, it introduces emotional intelligence, explaining why it is important and what it is. Finally, it makes the case for resilience as a superpower and outlines effective stress strategies. There are resources in the back of this book on the coaching and training available for the Resilient Leader System.

After two decades as a High-Performance Coach working with thousands of amazing individuals, distilling the best information from current research in the fields of resilience, emotional intelligence, leadership, and flow, I've outlined resilience as an effective solution for consistent high performance.

Is the Needed Change Stuck
in the Revolving Door?

The pressures continue in healthcare with technology, healthcare reform, and other complex issues that demand more and more from a system that has not made the well-being of its leaders and frontline professionals its priority. In order to have the stamina, mental focus, emotional flexibility and confidence to stand up to the tremendous demands in healthcare, professionals and especially leaders need to have tools to be effective in this high pressure environment.

Waiting until the weekend to rest up or catch up isn't enough to revitalize. With the stress reaction as a constant distraction, it is very challenging to operate at your best without a strategy in place. Too many leaders have disengaged, struggling to keep up with the demands from their people and from their administration. And when left unchecked, this stress reaction erodes the confidence in a leader and further interferes with effective decisions, communication, influence, and persuasion—tools of the high-performing leader.

Aging workforce, increased patient demand, healthcare reform, reimbursement changes, disengaged staff, and toxic culture are just a few of the many challenges facing leadership today. While leadership cannot directly impact the aging workforce, the increase in patient demands, or the challenges from healthcare reform, it is the job of leadership to impact the culture and staff in a positive way. In my opinion, the toxic culture and the disengaged staff are the biggest problems facing healthcare today.

For decades, healthcare has been bleeding the best and brightest from its ranks due to the toxicity within its culture. The nurses who stay are burning out, and the toxic nurses become toxic leaders pushing new, enthusiastic, and bright nurses through the revolving door. Look at these numbers: more than half of nurses with two years of experience leave their jobs. The RN Study has the career span of a nurse at eight years. Realistically, that is when nurses are just reaching their strides professionally with confidence in assessment skills, critical thinking, and judgement. New physicians, pharmacists, and other healthcare professionals depend on the judgement and clinical expertise of experienced nurses. The internet and supportive tools cannot make up the experience gap. Too many studies have shown that infection rates, mortality, and other indicators are negatively impacted without enough nurses.[1]

In a variety of studies, it is reported that for every percentage point of turnover, the cost to a hospital averages $300,000. The average turnover is 14%, translating to an annual turnover cost that exceeds $3,000,000.[2] This number does not account for the loss from disengaged staff who no longer care but still show up for work anyway. According to numerous authors and researchers, 70% of nurses have experienced bullying and 60% leave their jobs within six months after experiencing this toxic behavior. These numbers are just the tip of the iceberg. Error rates, waste due to ineffective processes, disgruntled employees all contribute to lower profits and ineffective systems.

With federal reimbursement soon to be based on performance, the time is now for leaders and organizations to learn to motivate and inspire their followers. I wrote this book for the individual; nurse, physician, healthcare professional, administrator and the leader who want to move beyond burnout, work life dissatisfaction, the toxic culture and learn to love their life again so they can continue to make a difference in the field. With every individual that wakes up to their own potential, they will transform the culture of organizations. It is my mission to offer a roadmap, a way up and out of this challenge, by focusing on the solution—and the solution lies in each individual. It is the superpower of resilience.

Numbers tell part of the story of the damages done to healthcare culture. For nurses and leaders, managing their roles as caregivers and their own wellbeing is a challenge that costs the majority of professionals their passion and capacity to care and compromises their commitment to the organization.[3] Without the tools, awareness, and ability to manage their own internal landscapes, how can healthcare professionals manage the culture?

Can healthcare afford to bleed millions of dollars in turnover and perpetuate a culture of disposable staff with its revolving door? Many executives are on "initiative overload," having lived through many cycles of shortages and programs to engage, recruit, and retain professionals with little perceived benefit. This doesn't make it okay to keep kicking the can down the road. The time to change is now. The place to start is within you. This book will show you how.

In order to solve the problem, one has to first define it rather than deny it. I see the problems in healthcare of overload, burnout, bullying, and turnover as symptoms of a cultural breakdown.[4] The change is going to take place within each individual who makes the decision to "do work" differently. Healthcare professionals cannot continue to treat themselves the same way as they always have, go through their days with no connection to meaning or purpose, and expect anything to change. This is the definition of insanity. In order to thrive and not just get through the day, you have to activate your resilience. The revolving door is a broken system, and it requires healthy, vibrant, and creative leaders to keep the very best professionals.

Resilient leadership is the motivating force for each individual to embrace change on a personal level in order to grow beyond burnout. Nurses, physicians, and leaders are burning out faster and losing interest in a role they once loved. Too many professionals who do stay in their jobs are cynical and disengaged. I have seen the revolving door and the consequences of it in the 40 years I have been a nurse. The level of dissatisfaction with the job and the lifestyle among all the professions in healthcare is actually staggering. I went to a large leadership conference recently and the sarcasm and lack of interest in innovative solutions took me aback. People walked around with blank stares looking overwhelmed and beat up.

We are in a perfect storm. As the general population ages, it requires more healthcare services and more caregivers to meet those demands—all at a time when the workforce is aging and a generation of professionals set to retire.[5] Healthcare reimbursement is changing again, and the continuum of care continues to shift away from the hospital and into the community. With a projected shortage of nurses on the horizon along with increased demands, where will the new leaders come from? Will healthcare evolve fast enough to stop the loss of great talent through the revolving door?

This book talks about resilience as a superpower, a new paradigm for high-performance leadership. All leaders can exercise a positive influence if they learn to operate from their authentic cores. An engaged leader will engage their followers and keep good staff. The main reason people leave is because they lose trust in their manager, according to Branheim in *7 Hidden Reasons People Leave.*[6] Frontline staff are craving leaders who truly understand and care about them, will mentor them, and will provide professional guidance and the moral strength to make fair and tough decisions. Resilience comes out of this core of authentic power; it is the partnership of mind, body, heart, and soul.

Power, influence, and authority have such negative connotations, and their essence is lost in the shadows of overbearing, manipulative, weak, and ineffective leaders. Most people have experienced dominating leaders who use their power over their people to demean them. Many have been the object of manipulation in the process of "influence." Far fewer have had the experience of a dynamic leader who understands the importance of an authentic presence that conveys confidence and authority.

If you are a leader or aspire to be one and want to develop your own authentic presence, then read on. I am honored to have you join me in the process of becoming the powerful presence healthcare needs you to be.

What do you think it costs your department when staff who have lost their ability to care about what they do show up for work?

How does this impact morale, productivity, patient outcomes, and the rest of the healthcare team?

Whose Responsibility Is Work-Life Balance?

It takes a village . . .

Accommodating work-life balance and safety on the job are key concerns in retaining nurses and improving their satisfaction. A study conducted by Dr. Jack Needleman and colleagues indicates that insufficient nurse staffing was related to higher patient mortality rates. They examined nearly 198,000 records of admitted patients and documentation from 177,000 eight-hour nursing shifts across forty-three patient-care units at large academic health centers. The data shows that the mortality risk increased 6% for patients when units were understaffed as compared with fully staffed units.[7]

Kaiser Permanente released the results from its National Survey on Consumers' Experiences with Patient Safety and Quality Information, revealing:

- 40% of Americans think that the quality of healthcare has worsened in the last five years.
- 74% of health professionals reported that the most important issues affecting quality of care were workload, stress, or fatigue.
- 70% of healthcare professionals reported too little time spent with patients as an issue impacting quality of care, and
- 69% reported too few nurses as the issue impacting quality of care.

These extensive studies point out that nursing care has a significant impact in patient outcomes with work life balance one of the biggest problems in the stability of the nursing work force. The demand for nurses is expected to grow by 26% by 2020, bringing the total number of job openings for nurses due to growth and replacements to 1.2 million.[8] In spite of the recent increase in employment due to the recession, large nursing shortages are still expected in the next decade.

The potential for a shortage is impacted by the aging population of nurses; nurses in their fifties are the largest segment of the nursing workforce, accounting for almost one quarter of the RN population.[9] The potential shortage is also fueled by the aging population in general, with the demand for care possibly exceeding supply of caregivers.[10] The ratio of potential caregivers to the elderly population will decrease by 40% between 2010 and 2030. Access to healthcare may be limited, unless the nursing population increases to meet the demand of the aging population.[11]

This nursing shortage puts more stress on nurses, which ultimately impacts patient care. In an original research study, Dr. Jeannie Cimiotti and associates found a significant association between high patient-to-nurse ratios and nurse burnout, with increased urinary tract and surgical site infections. The researchers found that increasing a nurse's patient load by just one patient was associated with higher rates of infection. The authors found an association between the wellbeing of nurses and successful patient outcomes.[12]

In another study reflecting the impact of increased patient-to-nurse ratios, the potential for burnout increased 23% and potential for job dissatisfaction increased 15%.[13] This means that almost half of nurses are negatively impacted as their patient loads increase.

The American Nurses Association (ANA) surveyed 4,614 nurses in 2011 about health and safety in their work environments. Acute and chronic stress from overwork continued to top the list. This study revealed that 53% of nurses work mandatory or unplanned overtime each month, down from 68% in 2001. Shifts are longer, with 56% saying their usual shift lasts ten or more hours, compared to 48% in 2001.[14]

Yes, these numbers tell a story and can be daunting. The truth is each individual is responsible for taking care of themselves, and there are things you can do, as their leader, to encourage this behavior. How does the Resilient Leader retain, develop, and recruit high-performing nursing staff? Here is one of my earliest lessons learned as a nurse starting out in the ICU: take your own pulse first before rushing into the emergency. This is so true for leaders; in order to lead your people, you have to lead yourself. Leaders set the emotional tone for their people. When communicating, the words you speak account for less than 10% of what is communicated; body language and non-verbal gestures carry the majority of the message. Just think about the last time you felt rested, refreshed, centered, and grounded. What was your message like, as opposed to when you felt overwhelmed and distracted by the stress reaction? Multiple researchers have found emotions are contagious, and as the leader, this is even truer: your team will resonate with your emotional tone, good or bad.

This is what makes self-awareness the critical foundation of emotional intelligence. Knowing what is going on inside of you gives you the power to leverage your own emotions and influence what is going on all around you. While it is the leader's job to ensure workplace conditions are safe and employees have the resources they need to do a good job, you cannot make your staff take better care of them. The most effective way to encourage this behavior is to model it in yourself. Yes, you can have staff development programs—I have taught many of them over the years. What I have found is that when leaders do not embrace the program personally, they will not hold staff accountable for high-performance behaviors like civility, healthy communication, and consistent patient outcomes. Then, the staff doesn't value the programs, and the programs are blamed for being ineffective. When you no longer allow yourself excuses for inconsistent performance, it will be hard to let your staff complain their way to low performance.

Reflection

Do you engage in a regular practice of self-care?

Describe.

Do you have a plan for your professional growth?

Describe.

The Disconnect: Denial and Deception

For all you Six Sigma enthusiasts, a miserable employee, particularly a miserable manager, is a defect.
—Jim Clifton, *The Coming Jobs War*[15]

Nursing leadership and hospital executives are disconnected from the problems of dissatisfaction and high stress among nurses and its impact on patient outcomes. A major survey found hospital administrators acknowledged that nurses may be dissatisfied *at other hospitals*, but not at their own hospitals![16]

Are executives dismissing the nurses' dissatisfaction at their facilities because of their own disconnect with their emotions and wellbeing? Or is self-deception a problem we all have as human beings? The short answer is yes to both. Having worked with thousands of people over twenty-plus years as a High-

Performance Coach, one of the most difficult problems in mentoring was opening people up to what the true problem really was—their own thought processes. The mind is excellent at telling you exactly what you want to hear. When you partner with the heart, body, mind, and soul to activate resilience, you are not as likely to fall into this trap. We will explore why (and how you avoid the trap) as we go through this book.

The "disconnect" is easy to understand when you look at the assumptions that operate within most:

- emotions should be neither seen nor heard;
- it is impossible to manage them, so it is best to ignore them;
- emotions get in the way of strategic decisions;
- emotions are a sign of weakness;
- emotions are not safe;
- and so many more excuses for not exploring one's emotional life.

Many leaders focused on six sigma and strategy believe that since emotions can't be measured, they can't be managed. For too many, emotions are the black box in the aircraft. You only look at them when there has been a crash or a tragedy. In reality, just think about your own experiences when emotions were ignored: they can be destructive.

It may be hard to quantify the value of self-awareness and the competency of emotional intelligence in your specific organization which may be why too many leaders fail to provide the training and mentoring needed for high-performance leadership. I understand. I like to keep focused on the goal—specific and measureable outcomes—and then look at the variables necessary to achieve that. Having a leader able to manage the stress and still communicate, think innovatively, and make good decisions is critical. This is often the source of errors, and where bottlenecks occur in operating more efficiently, poor communication is at the root cause. I believe an effective solution will integrate the practice of Six Sigma to define, measure, analyze, improve, and control with mentoring and training leadership in emotional intelligence to yield accountability for the best results and consistent high performance.

This disconnect (denial) is no longer a luxury healthcare can afford. The revolving door (and losing good people) is not a strategy; it is a side effect. There is enough evidence and data that supports the validity and necessity of providing training to develop self-awareness and emotional fitness.[17] More importantly, when leadership models this level of emotional competence and expects everyone to be accountable for their emotional intelligence, the culture shifts into high performance. Activating resilience sets the tone to strengthen performance; developing emotional intelligence will fortify the culture in encouraging civility, respect, caring for each other, and many other indicators of a high-performing culture.

This basic disconnect from the problem could be a matter of priorities. When asked if the problem of nursing shortages was real, 75% of surveyed executives responded *yes* but ranked the significance of the problem well below that of the problems of reimbursement, clinical quality, and regulatory issues.[18] This makes sense as the profit margins keep the doors open. Yet the leaching out of millions of dollars due to turnover, toxic culture, and errors that result from both makes this issue a priority when you take a hard look at the true cost of the revolving door. This type of overload and denial of the real problem is a short-sighted solution. Resilience sets up a cascade effect. As each healthcare leader is motivated to master his or her mindset and focus on solutions, this positive approach trickles down, empowering staff. There should be a standard of practice where professional are part of the solution, period.

As mentioned before, nurses provide care to sicker, needier patients with shorter hospital stays. The demands are high for everyone. Nurses need leaders who recognize the relationship between wellbeing and outcomes, and patients need staff who take care of themselves and are available and fully present to take care of them and their needs.

It should come as no surprise that the nursing leader is the direct link between nurse satisfaction and retention. One of the most prized "perks" for new nurses is having a manager who relates to them and provides mentoring. Leigh Branham, author of *The 7 Hidden Reasons Employees Leave*, states that the number-one reason that 80-90% of employees leave their organizations is a loss of trust and confidence in their immediate supervisors and senior leaders. He goes on to say that 70% of managers believe the reason employees leave is due to money, when in fact, it is due to the loss of trust.[19] The disconnect shows up again, creating a major breakdown between what employees claim is the reason for leaving and what managers believe. This makes it hard to find effective solutions when the problem is not well-defined.

Self-awareness is a critical factor in successful leadership and is a cornerstone of emotional intelligence. Knowing your strengths, weaknesses, and what triggers you while being able to identify your emotions and what to do about them in order to manage others is the essence of emotional intelligence. This includes being aware of what others might be experiencing. The stronger your emotional intelligence (EI), the less you fall into the trap of self-deception.

Since Daniel Goleman published *Emotional Intelligence and Why It Matters More than IQ* in 1995, there has been a flood of research and interest in how EI impacts life personally and professionally. Neither trendy, new, nor a fad, emotional intelligence represents the crucial intersection of personality, emotion, thoughts, and behavior in high-performance leadership. To simplify, EI is at the core of high performance and resilient leadership.

Emotions Are Not the Enemy: Awareness Is the Solution

Emotional intelligence is the awareness and management of one's internal landscape. This awareness is what increases the ability to engage and relate with others. This builds trust, empathy, effective communication, decisiveness, confidence, and, ultimately, an authentic presence. Chronic stress breaks down emotional intelligence, precipitating more reactive scenarios and potential emotional hijackings. This process of capitalizing on self-awareness, boosting confidence, and building effective communication skills develops your inner power and authority. This successful connection within enables you to exercise influence even in the face of stressful situations.

Emotions raise red flags in the culture of healthcare; too often, their expression is dramatic, harsh, and destructive. Emotional intelligence is not well understood, nor is it a competency displayed by healthcare professionals with bullying rampant in nursing and sarcasm, cynicism, and negativity the new normal in the workplace. This is rather shocking given the intimacy most healthcare professionals and especially nurses have with patients and families. It isn't a surprise that burnout and compassion fatigue are also epidemic.

Too many truly good nurses opt out of the field altogether rather than continue to be chewed up by a culture that does not value emotions. The reality of emotions is when they are ignored, they will show up in an exaggerated and excessive way. My book, *HEAL: Healthy Emotions. Abundant Life.*, goes into detail about the message of your emotions.[20] They really are your GPS: Guide for Professional Success! Emotions contain important and practical information about yourself and others. Emotions guide decisions and cannot be turned off (or on) when you go to work (or come home). They are designed to flow. It is nearly impossible to experience fulfillment if you have shut down your emotional flow. This is what happens in chronic, unchecked stress.

With a strong emotional intelligence, you can learn to use your emotions, tolerate stress, make decisions, act assertively, empathize, and be authentic in your interactions. Being emotionally fit means you can name your emotions and leverage them to achieve the outcome you really want. It doesn't mean you stop feeling. It means you stop reacting to what you are feeling.

Develop the habit of tuning in to identify basic feelings like anger, sadness, fear, and happiness, and you will keep from being hijacked emotionally, caught off-guard because your emotions were hidden and ignored. In my book, *HEAL: Healthy Emotions. Abundant Life.*, there is more detail on naming and claiming these basic emotions. Researchers have found that when you can name your emotion, you are less likely to overreact because of it. Having this conscious control over what you are feeling is a major step toward managing it.

Self-awareness is the cornerstone of high-performance leadership. It is your ability to identify your emotions and manage them in order to achieve your goal. Essential to self-awareness is an accurate inventory of your strengths, weakness, values, and goals. I have found most people short-change themselves with a list of their weaknesses with no strategy or confidence in their strengths. The Mastermind Program training helps you get in touch with what matters the most so you can operate from this strength.

Identifying and managing your emotions is critical for effective leadership. If you are in the throes of a stress reaction and reactive or operating on auto pilot because you are constantly "doing," you miss the subtleties in communication or the opportunities to advance your goals, and you disconnect from the purpose of what you are doing, missing out on a sense of satisfaction. You might rely on artificially scripted behavior to get you through and lose the momentum to build trust and connect with others. Interactions can become stale and meaningless. This is what causes disengagement. If leaders are operating on autopilot, can you expect their followers to show up giving 100 percent?

Emotional Intelligence: The Number-One Indicator of High-Performance Leadership

When Goleman analyzed the extensive research around emotional intelligence, he found that when leaders had a strong EI, they outperformed their annual goals by 20%.[21] What would a 20% increase in successful completion of your goals look like? This would put you ahead of the pack, position you for bonuses and promotion, and give you a sense of satisfaction and the reputation for getting things accomplished.

Your ability to manage your emotions and know what is really important to you helps you get what you ultimately want. After decades of research, the concept of emotional intelligence has matured. Roots of EI go back to the intelligence testing movement in the early 1900s when E. L. Thorndike, professor of educational psychology at Columbia University Teachers College, first identified social intelligence. From 1920 through the 1930s, attempts to measure the "ability to deal with people" essentially failed. For the next fifty years, behaviorists dominated the field of psychology, and the focus was on measuring IQ. In 1983, Howard Gardner, best known for his theory of multiple intelligences outlined in *Frames of Mind: The Theory of Multiple Intelligences*, was a major influence in resurrecting emotional intelligence. He included two types of personal intelligence in his theory: interpersonal and intrapersonal intelligences.

In the 1990s, Peter Salovey and John Mayer, colleagues at Yale at the time, published the influential and important article, "Emotional Intelligence." Their model distinguished emotional intelligence from social ability and emphasized the development of emotional skills to facilitate thinking. In 1995, Daniel Goleman wrote the book *Emotional Intelligence* and introduced emotional intelligence in the context of *performance*. Goleman was a science journalist and spread the word of the EI concept, adapting it to predict personal effectiveness. Since then, he has gone on to adapt his EI theory of performance to the workplace and beyond. He has written many more books on the subject.

With ongoing research, EI has passed several validation milestones and meets the criteria for an intelligence fitting within Gardner's personal intelligence. Instruments measuring aspects of EI are now on the market. Much has been accomplished in the past two decades to further EI as a predictor of performance, establishing the characteristics of outstanding performers.

Goleman defined the following five elements of emotional intelligence:

1. *Self-Awareness.*
   Do you know your emotions, values, and goals? Do you have an inventory of your strengths and weaknesses and know the impact you have on others?

2. *Self-Regulation.*
   Do you control yourself emotionally? Think before you act? Avoid swings of emotion—not too angry or jealous or hurt? Characteristics of self-regulation are thoughtfulness, comfort with change, integrity, and the ability to say no.

3. *Motivation.*
   Are you able to work for the long-term gain and defer immediate gratification? Characteristics include being highly productive, embracing challenges, and focusing on what is most effective.

4. *Empathy.*
   Do you identify with and understand the wants, needs, and viewpoints of those around you? Do you know the difference between sympathy and empathy? Sympathy

is "feeling one's pain." Empathy is acknowledging another's feelings and being willing to do something about it.

5. *Social Skills.*
   Are you easy to talk to? Are you a team player and interested in helping others move toward their goals?

Within these dimensions are additional skill sets that can be developed, such as assertiveness, stress tolerance, awareness, self-regard and more. Descriptions and exercises related to the sixteen dimensions of EI as reflected in the EQi 2.0 emotional intelligence assessment are detailed in the Resilient Leader Workbook and are part of the training and coaching program.

Reflection

How would you score your emotional awareness on a scale of one to ten, ten being very aware?

Emotional Hijacking (The Runaway Stress Reaction)

Stress is a primitive reaction. When stress is chronic and the ability to withstand stress (resilience) is underdeveloped, there are a number of consequences, such as the loss of emotional control, slower information processing, and a decrease in working memory, impacting long-range planning and creativity.

The number-one need today for leadership is creativity, and it is the first thing to go when stress is left unchecked.

Under stress, the amygdala—the part of the brain that monitors the environment for fear-inducing stimuli—is triggered, swamping more rational thought processes. This is the fast track of the stressed response.

Here is the reality of our nervous system: first you feel, then you think. The superpower of resilience decreases your reactivity, keeping you focused on what is most important and very clear. Building a capacity for stress allows you to rationally interpret feedback from your interactions along with stimuli coming from the environment. Stress tolerance means you operate more from your cortex and avoid the triggering of the primitive survival instinct of the amygdala firing. This is focus. This allows for systematic, methodical processing, critical thinking, and an evaluation process, making decisions better thought-out.

Chronic, unmanaged stress interrupts the ability to think clearly, remember, and retrieve important data. Many leaders, in hindsight, recognize that stress contributed to decisions that were not well thought-out or to emotional reactions uncharacteristic of their usual behavior. Instead of focusing on solutions, they are left with the challenge of damage control because of their reactions and poor decisions.

How much time is wasted on repairing the fallout from hijacked reactions?

Healthcare professionals would be well served to learn to activate resilience to move beyond burnout. This is even truer for nurses under thirty. In a survey of 843 direct-care hospital nurses, nurses under thirty were more likely to experience feelings of agitation and less likely to engage in self-management.

A leader who cannot think straight when under pressure will undermine teamwork, morale, and successful outcomes, adding to the stressors staff are already experiencing. This problem can be prevented with professional development. A resilient mindset is what produces a culture of high performance. Organizations that have clearly stated expectations and systems of accountability end up with the best retention and nurse satisfaction. This is what happened at St. Mary's Health Care in Athens, Georgia. The intentional effort to build a culture of quality based on hard work with an interactive leadership proved successful, decreasing turnover on one unit from 75% annually to a waiting list for potential employees. They focused on leadership development, improved communication from the top down, and daily interaction with the executive office.

The difference in high-performing leaders and those who aren't is resilience. When circumstances threaten business, resilient leaders will jump into action and initiate changes. Resilience encourages innovation and action and creates an intentional shift in the organization, such as setting up multidisciplinary teams and focusing on quality and better use of technology—all of which facilitate systematic changes such as new treatment or service protocols and better patient outcomes. This feeds continued productivity and high performance.

You Cannot Out-Perform Your Level of Wellbeing

Wellbeing is a measure of life satisfaction or contentment. How satisfied one is with oneself, one's lifestyle, and accomplishments helps to mitigate the negative effects of stress and contributes to building resilience. Wellbeing is enhanced with self-care. Self-care is something that is difficult for many caregivers, especially nurses. Nursing embodies the caregiver archetype and, as a result, abandons their own needs as they care for the patient. Without the ability to value themselves, nurses do not engage in self-care. Most nurses "know" they "should" take care of themselves, but they don't.

To understand and not do is to not understand.

This disconnect from one's wellbeing is reflected in a 2008 study published in the *Journal of the American Academy of Nurse Practitioners.* This study found that more than half of the 760 nurses who responded were overweight or obese. More than half of the respondents reported a lack of discipline to make lifestyle changes; there was not enough motivation to take care of themselves effectively.

Wellbeing is more than a feel-good concept; it is tied to performance and outcomes. It is the wild card that puts an organization ahead of the competition in consistent performance. Just think of your own experience when you did not get the right amount of sleep or may have over-indulged in some way the night before. What was the impact on your ability to be at the top of your game? How is your day without enough sleep or when you worry too much or fight with your teenager?

In today's workplace, 60% of the population is overweight, more than 50% do not exercise, and 25% smoke. A whopping 28% claim excellent health. This is the workforce today.

I am wondering if this is a time to ask the question: can this current culture within healthcare take care of patients when the providers have not yet made the connection that their own well-being impacts their ability to perform?

If not now, when?

Times have really changed. Communities are global, technology is outpacing the capacity of most to truly grasp it, and there is no way to speed up enough to catch up. Believe it or not, the most effective solution is to slow down and do less.

Ask yourself, in what way am I part of the solution (or the problem)?

Gallup has researched wellbeing and found that those reporting a high level of wellbeing out-perform by 200%. This is stunning. How is wellbeing *not* impacting the bottom line? I think the problem is that wellbeing is not understood or well-defined, making its achievement elusive. It is another measure like emotions that lives in the symbolic black box of the aircraft. You only explore it when there is a crash.

In the book *Well Being: The 5 Essential Elements*, Rath and Harter point out that wellbeing is not about happiness, and isolating one aspect of life like wealth, health (weight loss, blood pressure, smoking), status, or career can be detrimental to the overall experience of wellbeing. This is because aspects of life do not exist in isolation. Finding balance between work, home, and professional and personal relationships requires attention and a strategy. It is an ongoing process. First, you have to have the energy to focus on it and follow through.

Wellbeing is not easily defined. The discussion of what constitutes wellbeing has been going on since philosophers like Aristotle contemplated the essence of human existence. Gallup identifies five areas of life (career, social, community, physical, financial) that, when fulfilled, create an overall sense of wellbeing. Others relate wellbeing to subjective feelings like happiness and satisfaction along with indicators like blood pressure, BMI, and activity levels. As individuals, we all need to figure out what wellbeing means for us.

As a leader, what are the wellbeing indicators for your department and your people? Attitude, engagement, and motivation along with other indicators like error rate, absenteeism, and retention all can be factored in when evaluating the wellbeing in your department.

As I explored the field of wellbeing, I found some common ground among the authors, researchers, and scientists. Based on that and my work with thousands of amazing clients over twenty years, I developed my own five-element Wellbeing Map that includes the following dimensions of wellbeing: energy (vibrant health), connections (relationships), contribution (meaning and purpose), ability to keep going (resilience) and growth (self-care).

Reflection

Take the Wellbeing Assessment in the back of the book and plot your score on the spider graph. Where are you out of balance? Then, answer the three questions.

What Does It Mean to Work SMART?

Ultimately, this book is about uncovering limiting beliefs about work, yourself, success, and abundance. Chronic stress robs you of creativity, focus, and the awareness of possibility. When you embrace beliefs that will validate you, your strengths, and your purpose, you are more likely to go through your day in flow. This superpower is talked about later in the book.

You can Google, "Work smart, not hard," and find many time management tips and resources. I have taken this model and changed it to reflect a true energy management system versus focusing solely on the limited perspective of time. Time will always be finite and limited in nature. Focusing on limitations is a set-up to feel like there is never enough of anything, including time. Working SMART focuses on your ability to master your energy for a consistent level of performance.

Stress sets up a false sense of urgency and robs you of the clarity to find the best solution while using up vital energy as you spin your wheels. When you activate your resilience, you operate "efficiently" from your best internal resources. You will learn how to do this in this program.

Use this model to set goals and make your choices and decisions (also see *Fig. 1*).

S **Specific**. Make your choices, decisions, and goals very clear. Know what you want. Focus on what is important, not what is most urgent.

M **Measurable**. What you measure, you control. Be sure to understand the impact of your choices and decisions and quantify the cost of them.

A **Authentic**. Make choices and decisions that remain true to your goals, purpose, and values. Be aware when other people are pushing their needs on you.

R **Risky**. Make choices and decisions that stretch you and take you out of your comfort zone. When you are clear, focused, and aware of the impact, you control the risk. Growth equals success.

T **Timely**. Your choices, decisions, and goals need to have a deadline and or expiration date.

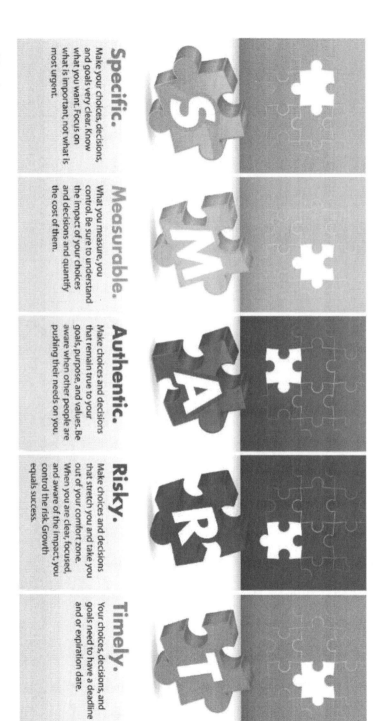

Fig. 1

Specific.
Make your choices, decisions, and goals very clear. Know what you want. Focus on what is important, not what is most urgent.

Measurable.
What you measure, you control. Be sure to understand the impact of your choices and decisions and quantify the cost of them.

Authentic.
Make choices and decisions that remain true to your goals, purpose, and values. Be aware when other people are pushing their needs on you.

Risky.
Make choices and decisions that stretch you and take you out of your comfort zone. When you are clear, focused, and aware of the impact, you control the risk. Growth equals success.

Timely.
Your choices, decisions, and goals need to have a deadline and or expiration date.

Resilience: The Superpower
for High Performance

Resilience is defined as the ability to recover quickly, to bounce back from frustration or failure. As healthcare professionals, you have seen numerous examples of patients and families triumphing over difficult conditions. Resilience often shows up during the most extraordinary of times. It is a trait everyone can access, yet many do not. This program is designed to assist you in accessing this superpower.

Being resilient doesn't mean you do not experience any distress; it means you keep going despite the challenges. Leaders, you would be well served to develop your own in order to overcome the complexity and ambiguity that is the fabric of healthcare leadership today.

Resilience is the inner game of success which drives behavior. It is your internal guidance system that draws from your body, mind, heart, and soul to ensure your success. Ask yourself the following:

- Do your daily dietary choices support vibrant energy and stamina?

- Do your thoughts move you closer to your goals, or are you stuck in fear and self-doubt?

- Do your beliefs about yourself and what is possible line up with your goals?

- Are you motivated to avoid something or focused on moving toward what you want?

When you embrace resilience as a superpower, you make the choice in the face of challenge to keep moving forward, as opposed to giving up and feeling like a victim to what is happening all around you. The nature of resilience is to believe you are capable of growing and changing rather than believing you are limited in your resources, drive, and strength.

Three Myths That Get in the Way of Activating Your Resilience

1. "I work best under pressure."

The stress reaction is a hardwired reaction that has been part of our nervous system for the last 100,000 years. Once this flight, fight, or freeze reaction is engaged, rational, logical, and critical thinking is suspended. This reaction is emotional in nature and reactive and obliterates creative problem solving. The problem is that today, this primitive reaction is engaged more easily as technology takes over more and more of our attention and many people are stuck in the throes of this reaction, not realizing they are operating on autopilot.

Over 95% of the choices most people make during the course of their days are made on autopilot. This means that choices are reactive; the focus is on what is most urgent versus most important, and fear often drives decisions. When you tell yourself there is never enough time or resources, it is easy to feel resentful, angry, or procrastinate. This triggers other thoughts to support this feeling of being a victim and powerless. First, you need to recognize you are operating on autopilot and shift into a mindful and aware state.

One of the dimensions in emotional intelligence that we cover in the program is "Reality Testing." How tuned in are you to what is happening and the impact of what is happening? When you are caught in the chronic stress reaction, most people make decisions in the moment without fully evaluating the consequences.

Procrastination is a default mode for people who tell themselves they work best under pressure. This is also one of the favorite ways you can stay a step ahead of feeling like an imposter. Either way, this book has alternatives for you to break out of this pattern.

2. "You can never be too prepared."

When you are caught up in chronic stress, most people try to outrun it. Working harder to stay ahead of the demands increases your pressure and decreases your sense of satisfaction. This can lead to burnout or exhaustion. Problem solving is one of the dimensions in emotional intelligence that we cover in the Resilient Leader System (RLS). This helps you clearly define the problem and work through the process of setting it up. This will keep you focused and clear as well as help you communicate with your team.

Are you caught up in over preparing because you do not feel capable? This is one of the four traps researchers Clance and Imes identified in the imposter syndrome.[22] Working through an accurate inventory of your strengths and learning to own them is at the core of the Resilient Leader Program. This is the antidote for this irrational fear of being found out as a fraud.

3. "You can never think too much about a problem."

Great thinking is a habit that you can develop. It is what separates conventional, linear thinking from the ability to embrace complexity. In my Integrative Health Practice, I would encourage clients to shift their thinking from simple cause and effect to consider how aspects of their life impact their problem and solution; this often meant the difference between vibrant health and just getting through their day. Good thinking solves problems. You need good input in order to have creative solutions so make it a habit to expose yourself to positive ideas. You may even spend time just thinking through all aspects of the problem and its solutions. This is not the same thing as worrying.

Overthinking and worry are not strategies to handle pressure. They are the default for a stress reaction gone wild. Chronic stress reduces the ability to think clearly and broadly, instead keeping you focused on a small area. Here is where trying too hard only gets in the way of clear, focused problem solving and decisions.

Quick Tip: If you are feeling worried or fearful, you are overly focused on the problem. Keep your eye on solutions, and you will empower yourself and others.

Developing impulse control and stress tolerance are two of the sixteen dimensions that help to manage the pressure of stress. The RLS Workbook includes details on each of the sixteen dimensions of emotional intelligence.

Reflection

How could your life look with less drama and chaos from stress?

The Power of Belief

Without a humble but reasonable confidence in your own powers, you cannot be successful or happy.
—Norman Vincent Peale

Optimism is a really important aspect of resilience. In the book *Resilience: The Science of Mastering Life's Greatest Challenges*, the authors, Southwick and Charney, asked Special Forces instructors if their soldiers tended to be more optimistic than pessimistic. The answer was resoundingly, "Optimistic." They noted how contagious an attitude is and said they could not afford risking the entire team's attitude if one of them became really negative.

As a leader, do you have a standard for attitudes? What if you required your team to be optimistic in order to work with you?

While genetics play a role in whether you are naturally optimistic—just like with high blood pressure and diabetes—there are things you can do every day to increase your optimism. Seligman in *Authentic Happiness* talks about increasing positive thoughts and refuting negative ones. In the Resilient Leader System, we cover strategies that help you do this. The first step is to become aware of your attitude, thoughts, and self-talk. Become an observer of your conversations. If you feel worried, fearful, or have more doubt, you are focusing on the problem rather than the solution. Resilient leaders acknowledge the problem and spend more time on the solution. This is empowering for you and everyone around you.

Optimism is not an "everything is fine" attitude. It is realistic and recognizes the challenges in front of you and plans for them. What makes one optimistic is the confidence in oneself to handle those challenges. Confidence comes from a belief in oneself and grows when you move through challenges. It comes from mistakes, failures, and difficulty. It is the direct result of continuing to get back up after every challenge. It does not come from playing it safe and not stretching yourself beyond your comfort zone. Resilience takes that confidence and increases its power with persistent and deliberate focus on the ultimate goal.

The Resilient Leader System will help you challenge beliefs you have about yourself and what you think is possible for you personally and professionally. This is important because most beliefs you have about yourself were created very early, before the age of five. These beliefs are not automatically updated with your accomplishments. Beliefs are formed at a very early age; when your early beliefs are limiting, it doesn't matter what the objective facts may be. This may explain why so many people feel like an imposter or they are faking it, even after great achievement. This confidence gap is one of the biggest challenges I have seen in my practice, getting in the way of results you want on the job and having the quality relationships you want both at home and at work. Valerie Young writes about the "imposter syndrome" in her book, *The Secrets of Successful Women*, and states that while this fraud fear affects more women, men are also relating more and more to this.

It may surprise you to learn that Maya Angelou was a member of the imposter club. "I have written eleven books," she said, "but each time I think, 'Uh-oh, they're going to find out now. I've run a game on everybody, and they're going to find me out.'" Albert Einstein was also thought to struggle with this near the end of his life.

I cannot count the number of amazing individuals I have coached who were also struggling with this fear; there were more that did than did not. This book and program is in part a solution to feeling like an imposter by owning your strengths and shifting your mindset to finally embrace a true confidence.

Healthcare cannot afford to lose another person's big ideas because he or she played it small.

The beliefs one holds are designed to ensure survival, just like emotions and the stress reaction. *Just surviving,* as a standard for your day (life) limits the potential that is available for problem solving, relationships and performance. The primitive survival instinct that drives the nervous system can be thought of as an operating system, like Windows or Apple and it has been hundreds of thousands of years without an upgrade to the internal nervous system. This makes resilience the timely upgrade to learn to thrive in your life.

Beliefs are not easily changed because beliefs are the survival tool the nervous system uses when it cannot sense what is safe and not safe. Beliefs are not subject to facts but rather based entirely on the need to survive. In the formative years, parents and culture were necessary for survival, and what they believed about you mattered more than anything. Most people grow up treating themselves the way they were treated. Changing your beliefs today means you recognize that to continue to play it small, you miss out on the possibilities that are waiting for you, and so does your team.

The Resilient Leader System includes the Mastermind Program which takes you through the process of owning your confidence (strengthening emotional intelligence) so you will lead from an authentic and truly inspiring place.

If resilience contributes to success and is actually vital for a fulfilled life, why do most people ignore this superpower?

Super Tip: On a Count of Four, Breathe!

Breathe in on a count of four. Hold it for a count of four. Exhale on a count of four. Repeat three times. Next, breathing normally, bring up feelings of appreciation and gratitude and let this feeling flood your entire being for fifteen seconds. Continue to breathe while you enjoy this appreciation. By doing this, you are building your stress tolerance and activating your resilience. This takes practice and, just like any exercise, will have cumulative benefit, increasing your stress tolerance.

Do this practice for three minutes five times a day. Use your timer throughout the day to remind yourself. When you practice, set the timer for three minutes.

Authentic Presence: Transforming Conflict into Opportunity

au·then·tic adjective \ə-'then-tik, ȯ-\
: having authority; possessing inherent authority; duly authorized; authoritative [23]

When you are stressed, overwhelmed, and distracted by a false sense of urgency, it is tempting to micromanage, dominate, or control because of the pressure. This is a fear-based activity and limits your ability to perform. As you develop self-awareness, one of the competencies in EI (emotional Intelligence), you will have the opportunity to confront your fears and let go of the barriers to professional growth.

Being "authentic" doesn't mean sharing every thought or feeling that comes into your mind. It does mean you are consistent in your values, behavior, and thoughts. It is the standard to which you hold yourself accountable.

The following are a few characteristics I found in the literature that describe an "authentic leader":

- ✓ Good listener

- ✓ Passionate and purpose-driven

- ✓ Practical

- ✓ Honest, forthright

- ✓ Shows courage

- ✓ Has the ability to simplify and explain

- ✓ Walks the walk; has integrity

The word *authentic* has its roots in the word, authority—to be aligned with one's inner power. William James talks about authenticity as knowing what makes one feel the most alive and real. Bill George wrote the book *Authentic Leadership* and says being authentic is the true essence of leadership. He identifies great leaders as being autonomous and highly independent.[24] These are dimensions within EI that enable you to make tough decisions.

What does it mean to live (and lead) authentically? It is a phrase that is tossed around a lot, but it is much more than a cliché. To be authentic means you know what your values are and choose to live by them. You are aware of your strengths and your weaknesses. Too often, leaders feel they have to be perfect and overly confident, acting like they know everything they need in order to gain respect of their followers and other leaders in the organization. Accepting your weaknesses is not the same as dwelling on your weaknesses, apologizing for them, or leading with them underneath excuses. To be authentic, one acknowledges one's gifts and strengths *along with* weaknesses, knowing that complete self-acceptance is what keeps one centered. Changing who you are for approval from others is precarious and only increases the level of stress. It is what contributes to the lack of fulfillment in one's job.

This level of self-awareness comes from a strong foundation of emotional intelligence. George talks about the need for effective leaders and how hard it can be to look within. In the Resilient Leader System, you will have the opportunity to connect with your own story around leadership, helping you better understand who you are and what your true style of leadership is. This is building your foundation of emotional intelligence.

How does being authentic transform conflict into opportunity?

To be authentic, one has to take responsibility for self-growth. The more you accept challenges, admit defeat, and walk through uncertainty, the greater trust you will have in yourself, the more you will establish trust with those around you, and the more empathy you will have with others. Being able to operate from your core—who you really are—actually reduces conflict in the long run, opening doors for relationships that would not otherwise be possible.

Other Superpowers You Cannot Lead (Live) Without

You will support your resilience by engaging in the following superpowers. These were first introduced in my book, *HEAL, Healthy Emotions. Abundant Life.,* and are reprinted here. The stress strategies in this book will help you to de-stress so you can better engage these powers.

The Power of Now

"This moment is all you really have. The past is over and the future not here yet. In this moment there is unlimited possibility."

The point of power is in the present moment. Where do you live? In the past, replaying old arguments or scenes in your mind, or in the future, wishing and hoping for the outcome you want? Meanwhile, what has become of the present moment?

Being present has never before been so difficult. The new normal of compulsively checking emails, texts, and social media has destroyed focus and replaced it with a dazed and disengaged presence. This increases irritability and frustration. This translates into feeling more stress and tension in your body, causing more distraction. This vicious cycle is the treadmill of daily life for many people. This is the biggest energy drain today because, in the dazed and distracted zone, you make poor food choices, you make mistakes (maybe even fatal ones), and you miss out on real experiences that might boost your spirit or help you feel good. Instead, you barely remember what you're doing.

This level of distraction is complicated by your brain under the influence of the stress reaction, communicating sensations and triggers to your body and mind. This hijacking is what distorts the present and keeps you locked into reactions. Your primitive brain likes to categorize your experiences into good, bad, right, wrong, painful, or pleasurable, and this type of thinking then dominates your rational mind. You can unhook from this by practicing mindfulness and learning to be present in the moment. This practice will expand your possibilities and release the tension, worry, and dread that comes from your primitive brain being in charge.

This *superpower of now* is the ability to bring your attention to the present moment and focus on what you are doing right now without judgment, your mind wandering, or other competing thoughts. It takes practice. It is worth the effort. This is the practice of mindfulness.

Begin now.

Let's say you are at work in a staff meeting. You don't like being there because it takes time away from finishing up your work. In the past, to avoid feeing the resentment, your mind wandered, and you would think about your next vacation or some place you loved visiting. Since you have learned about the *Superpower of Now*, you want to deliberately bring your attention to the meeting. Act as if it is the very first time you have been in the meeting. What do you notice? Your only job is to observe. Let any thoughts drift away.

Use this technique with any person, place, or situation, telling yourself it is the very first time you have seen or heard or been there. Just observe and notice. What is different? This ability to reboot your attention to see more of what is around you keeps you from being complacent, distracted, smug, or stuck. It is easy to block out small details that can be quite meaningful when caught up in the "doing" of daily life. Compulsive doing can create an attitude of, "I can do it all," "I know everything there is to know," or, "Nothing ever changes." There is more opportunity around you than you realize because most people are caught up in a habit living life distracted. Bring your attention into the moment, and then learn to power up your thoughts.

The Power of Thought

"Whatever you think about, you bring about."

It is estimated that your mind goes through 50,000 to 80,000 thoughts per day. That is between 2,000 and 3,300 per hour. Your brain weighs three pounds and has 30 billion neurons, powerhouse cells that analyze, dream, plan, remember, and process 30 billion bits of information per second. You have at your disposal a supercharged miracle that can leave even the best computer in the dust. Unfortunately, most people don't bother to turn it on and simply go through their days on autopilot.

You may think that the thought you had to get that double mocha chocolate latte was original; however, it is a reaction to the stressful interaction with your teenager and is now a habit that is triggered when you feel that tension in your neck. The same is true with 90% of the thoughts you think.

Many years ago, I had a client who was a CNO (Chief Nursing Officer). He came to me to improve his communication skills. He was seen as aloof and detached by nurses. He said that he never felt comfortable interacting with the nurses and felt all they did was complain. He shared that early in his life, his family moved around a lot. He never made good friends and felt like an outsider in school. He had not thought of that until we explored his current hesitation to interact more with the nurses. His thoughts are based on forty-year-old data of moving frequently and never feeling comfortable around people—data that is no longer relevant.

Is your supercomputer being powered by outdated and old software? Are you on autopilot? Question yourself, and ask why you are thinking or doing what you are doing. Do you really want that pie, burger, fries, (you name it)? Do you really want to drink thirty-two ounces of soda a day? Do you want to follow through with that Facebook post? What are you doing that is based on old programming?

Change your thoughts, and you will change your life. This is my favorite topic: powering up your mindset. I grew up in a home steeped in despair and negativity. I wanted so much to go beyond the limitations my parents set for themselves. I did not have the advantages of money as we lived paycheck to paycheck, and I was determined to find a way to break out of this limiting situation. Early on, I learned that when you master your mindset, you master life. I am passionate about sharing this with you because the answer to any problem is to use your thoughts deliberately.

Whatever you set out to do begins first with a thought. Edison did not set out to create the light bulb with the idea he would fail. Henry Ford believed in his idea to create an automobile for the masses and turned down a secure lucrative position to pursue his dream. He succeeded because he was determined. He is famous for saying, "Whether you think you can or you think you can't, you are right."

Think about your own life. Think about a time you succeeded at something. What were your thoughts at the time? Now, go to a time when you failed or did not meet your goal. What were your thoughts like? Everything begins with a thought. What do you think about your life? Is this the thought you want to power your ship?

In our programs, we provide audio and video to take you through the process of visualization, intention, and relaxation. Learning to deliberately use your thoughts to create the life you really want is your ticket to emotional freedom.

What is the most important thought you need to change in your life in order for your life to change?

Knowing that everything begins with a thought, start to tune in to what you are thinking. Whenever a negative or limiting thoughts shows up, immediately change it to one that is positive. If you have trouble with a person at work and tend to grumble about having to work with that person, *Ugh, I really do not want to work with her; my day is shot,* can become, *I am open to great possibilities working with this person; I choose to shift my attitude.*

Keep in mind it is easier to maintain a positive attitude than correct a negative one. Changing negative thoughts can be done, and is well worth it. After all, who do you prefer to be around—someone complaining or someone who is positive? The first step to changing your negative thoughts is to recognize you are stuck in this habit. Negativity is a habit. Keep a Thought Journal: note the day, time, what you are doing, what you have eaten, and who else is around. This will help you recognize when you feel negative and tune in to your thoughts. Are you focused on a disaster scenario or focused on a problem? Immediately shift your mind and imagine the scene as you want it to happen. What is important here is to realize you have control over what and how you think.

Thought Reboot

Engaging the *superpower of thought* is doing exactly that: taking control of your thoughts. Set up a new habit of affirmations. Use the card deck that comes with the Heal Program and sprinkle them around your home, car, or office. When you brush your teeth, get in the habit of repeating affirmations to yourself. Think of other times during the day when you intentionally focus your thoughts. This becomes your new habit. Your thoughts are influenced by your emotions. Often, changing your thoughts will shift your feelings and mood. The more you focus on the positive, the happier you will feel. Changing your thoughts is not something you do once and then forget about it. It is a process you will continue to do, and it gets easier every time you set your intention.

Thoughts come out of the unconscious part of your mind, and your conscious mind is its gatekeeper. The more self-aware (conscious) you are, the greater control you have over what you think. Being aware—*using the superpower of now*—you are able to protect your unconscious mind from the predators of fear, doubt, and other influences that come from people, places, and situations. Advertising on TV, radio, and the internet are constantly trying to instill an urgent need and desire for the product through emotionally charged images. The unconscious is more susceptible to suggestion during very stressful times or in heightened emotional conditions like fear and panic. Staying present rather than distracted by the stress reaction will help you keep positive thoughts front and center and the negative ones at bay.

What are the attitude adjustments you can make to transform the outcomes in your life?

The *superpower of thought* is your opportunity to change the outcome and the trajectory of your life—one thought at a time.

The Power of Flow
"It is the journey that counts"

Have you ever gotten so involved that you lose track of time and nothing else matters? This is the *superpower of flow.* This effortless concentration and enjoyment is achieved when engaged in an experience like singing in a band, playing chess or poker, golfing, dancing, skiing, reading, painting, and even working. Some people call it "being in the zone." Athletes, musicians, actors, and others talk about this experience of effortless action as the best times of their lives.

Many years ago, I worked with a physician who loved what he did, and in spite of the long hours and the demands of the job, he rarely felt exhausted. His wife was disappointed that he did not spend more time with her, and we worked on creating more balance. Since he had already learned to embrace this superpower of flow in his professional life, I helped him use this in his personal life.

What if you could create this experience deliberately?

Mihaly Csikszentmihalyi, author of *Flow: The Psychology of Optimal Experience*, writes that it is this experience of flow and not happiness that makes for an excellent life. In his research, Csikszentmihalyi found the flow experience took the individual into a different reality, opening them up to greater discovery.[25] Flow happens when you are focused and challenged and you enjoy the experience. It does not happen when you are passively involved or disengaged. In fact, one of the best ways to get into flow is to embrace challenge.

You will achieve FLOW when you:

- ✓ Focus.

- ✓ Love what you are doing.

- ✓ Own your strengths.

- ✓ Welcome the challenge.

The opposite of flow is boredom, a state where you are not stretched and are operating below your ability. You can go from boredom to flow simply by increasing your focus and challenging yourself to learn a new skill or set a more difficult goal and enjoying the process. Flow happens when you engage yourself and stretch. Flow feels really good. It is enjoyable, and it can be cultivated. Just as you learned to deliberately bring yourself into the moment and direct your thoughts, the next step is to build in a challenge for yourself in your day. Flow requires you to invest your attention and be willing to push yourself. Success is when you meet any challenge with the same or greater response. Flow is your ticket to success. Shift your thoughts about the challenges facing you. Go after the skills you need to meet the challenge and enjoy the process.

Are you on autopilot and just drifting through your day?

To get into flow, you have to be willing to focus. Today more than ever, focus is a challenge. Spend time away from technology, read, or concentrate on something for twenty uninterrupted minutes. Practice the tips in this book, acknowledge and release your emotions, and always remember to breathe.

The *superpowers of Now and Thought* will help you bring yourself into the present. To engage flow, ask yourself what new things you can learn every day to make your work better. Make it a contest or experiment, and enjoy the challenge of finding solutions. Anytime you focus on the solution, you energize your confidence. When you focus on the problems, you are eroding your confidence.

Work Reboot

Practice active listening to hear what your coworkers are really saying, and avoid quick judgments and overreaction. Learn additional clinical skills, and increase your interest and enthusiasm for work. Talk with your manager to find out what expectations he or she has for your job. Express your appreciation for your manager. Take a moment, breathe deeply, and relax before you go into your patients' rooms. Be present, and let them feel you are right there with them. This mindfulness increases your observation skills and reduces their anxiety. This is a win-win.

How will you invest your attention in your work life and increase your flow experience?

By deliberately focusing your attention on what you can do to improve your work life (versus complaining about the job), you take charge of your thoughts and the ultimate outcome. This is operating in the superpower of Flow. The superpowers build on themselves and overlap, so the more you engage in one, the more it helps you with the others.

The Power of Love
"Love is the only thing that increases as you give it away"

Love is the most powerful force in the world. When you have it, you feel like the world is your oyster. When you do not have it, the world looks like your enemy. Most people end up chasing love in some form or other without realizing that they themselves are the vessel through which love flows.

I want you to be willing to allow more love in your life. This book has been about opening up to your emotions and the deeper wisdom that is available to you. It is about letting the emotions flow rather than having them bottleneck and shut down your life force. Disappointment, betrayal, and hurt takes its toll physically, mentally, and spiritually. Loving yourself is the doorway to having more love in your life from others.

Think about love as the essential life force. This life force (vibration) is the substance of everything around you. To create more of what you want in your life, the vibration of love has to flow more easily. When you shut down this vibration of energy, you limit what is possible in your life. To have more abundance in your life, you want to focus on the life-giving energy of love rather than the life-draining energy of desire.

I am not talking about the love that comes from your own personality; rather, it is the Divine Love that is the source of all creation. This Love is from God. It is the highest frequency of energy. When engaged, it changes matter, creates something new, breaks through patterns, and lifts up all consciousness.

It is hard to conceptualize. We all start out with a model of love that came from our parents or earliest experiences in family and culture. We love ourselves the way we were loved, and way too often, this is the problem. We recreate the pattern of love we received, and this pattern dictates our lives. When inadequate, life ends up "feeling" inadequate, and the chase begins for love and happiness, thinking that things, people, or status are going to fill this longing inside.

Thinking you are doing the best thing, you might shut down to "protect" yourself from further disappointment, hurt, or betrayal. After all, being vulnerable is scary. Think back to the boundary section. Boundaries are also about what you allow into your life. Being rigid and blocking any opportunity for disappointment also shuts down the possibility for something good to happen. Learning to listen in and honor the message of your emotions will help you to have more fluid boundaries and stay open to the *super power of Love*. When your heart shuts down and you disconnect from hope and the ability to forgive, you diminish the capacity to join with the Divine energy and create abundance.

You are a co-creator of your life, and *love* is what magnetizes this process.

I could go on and on writing about what love is, but to truly understand, it has to be experienced. Forgiveness, gratitude, appreciation, awe, humility, and faith are all stepping stones to opening up one's heart and soul to this universal force. Engaging the other Superpowers are going to open you to receive more love.

The first feelings of love are felt in the heart. Since ancient times, the heart center has been considered significant. This reference is not about the physical organ of the heart but rather the energy center of the heart. The heart chakra is the fourth of seven energy centers that make up your energy field. The heart has the strongest energy field of all. It is this vortex of Divine energy that serves as the center through which everything is created.

You are pure energy. It is true. The MRI, PET scan, and other diagnostic tests use the energy field to diagnose disease. Traditional medicine does not yet use the energy field to heal. We are all made up of atoms that contain the energy field for our identities. The more consciously aware you are, the more you magnetize your own field. Think of love as the super magnet. Love heals. Think about those times when you were comforted by someone you love. Healing, wasn't it? Now, imagine Divine Love, infinitely more powerful, comforting you. This Love is available to you all the time. Ask. Be open. Receive.

Are you open to receive love from the universe/God?

Love Reboot

For more love to come into your life, be willing to send more love out to others. Practice sending love to your immediate family, and imagine a circle of love surrounding them. Extend that love beyond your home to your neighbors. Practice this feeling for fifteen to twenty seconds, and work up to a minute or longer. As you practice, you will open your heart to receive more and more love yourself and bring into your life more loving people and circumstances.

The disappointment, betrayal, or heartbreak can be released quickly using Tapping. I have used it with thousands of people and have seen it work quickly. Tapping is effective, even if you do not believe it will work. While it is understandable to shut down, it is what keeps you from receiving the blessings that have your name on them.

Did you know the God Self within you is *you*? There is no place where God leaves off and you begin. Begin a practice of loving yourself from the depths of your *inside* to your complete *outside*. Learning to love yourself is what will ensure you live a balanced and fulfilled life. Make it a point to pour out Love to yourself and extend this to anyone with whom you have conflict, disagreement, or hurt.

Enjoy spreading love. It is the one thing that increases as you give it away.

The Power of Focus

"success is directly related to your ability to focus"

It is a skill you can develop—possibly the most significant. In the Age of Distraction, everything is competing for our attention, and the inability to focus has become quite a disadvantage.

Do you know what is most important for you to focus on at work? Do you have priorities for your family? Are you clear on your values? Have you defined your personal goals? Getting clear takes time. I highly recommend you set aside time to think this through. When you are clear about what is important and what you need to focus on, it is easier to say no and set boundaries.

Here are a few strategies to support this *superpower of focus*.

1. Evaluate your habits. Do you have habits that are aligned with your goals? 90% of your behavior is automatic and based on habits. Too often, these habits get in your way of performance and productivity and cost you precious time and energy. Getting derailed because you stayed up late again and now can't focus on what is in front of you is a habit you can change with this "Cost-Benefit" Analysis.

   Work through it with the chart in *Fig. 2.*

2. Identify your strengths. Operate from your brilliance rather than making excuses because of your weaknesses. In the Resilient Leader System, you will go through a series of assessments that will help you identify your strengths. What comes easily for you? What do you do that others find difficult? Working with a coach will cause a dramatic shift in your ability to own your talents and gifts. Having true confidence is one of the biggest gains my clients have as a result of coaching.

3. Use visualization to see yourself achieving your goal. Set up fifteen to thirty minutes at the start of every day to pray, feed your spirit, read inspiration, define your priorities for the day, and visualize your goals. Visualization is detailed in the section on Stress Strategies.

Cost Benefit Analysis of Your Habits		
Habit that Blocks Success	Successful Habit	Strategies to Support New Habit
Procrastination Cost 1. Miss deadlines 2. Lose credibility 3. Feel overwhelmed 4. Miss opportunities for promotion	**Focus and Finish; Improved Follow Through** Benefit 1. Greater confidence 2. More time to spend on planning 3. Seen as an effective leader and problem solver.	1. Schedule time to read emails and texts. Reduce the distractions during the day. 2. Delegate the jobs that are not part of my role. 3. Schedule time to work on projects and limit activities that detract from their completion.
Implementation Date: July 29		

Fig. 2

4. Get the help you need. If you are crunched for time, what can you hire out so you can focus on your biggest priority? Hire a cleaning service, painter, landscaper, or other services so you can enjoy time with your family. What can you delegate and or train your assistant to do so you can focus on what really matters at work? Way too often, the reason assistants or delegation don't work

is because of poor communication. You have to be clear and concise when you state your expectations.

5. Avoid the "If Only" trap. Rumination over what might happen will waste your time and drain your energy. It will dampen your desire to find creative solutions. This trap is also rooted in regrets. Work on building good habits, and you will not have to spend time focusing on what "coulda, shoulda, woulda" happened.

The Five-Minute Shift: Stress Strategies

In order to activate resilience, you have to practice strategies that will unhook you from the reactive nature of the stress reaction. In this section, I have outlined several strategies that are proven to work within minutes. With regular use, you can build your resilience "muscle" and increase your tolerance of stressful situations.

Here are three steps to success:

1. Familiarize yourself with all of them. Use them all at least twice.

2. Start using them when you are relaxed and rested.

3. Do something every day, even if you do not feel you need it.

It is important to remember that stress is the new normal and in order to become resilient, you will have to practice at least one of these methods on a regular basis. You cannot think your way out of a stress reaction, and when you ignore what can happen, you leave yourself vulnerable to a hijacking. Just as in the Super Tip, "On a Count of Four, Breathe," these strategies can be incorporated into your day and are accomplished in minutes. As I mentioned, it is your desire for successful leadership and a fulfilled life for yourself that will fuel your decision to use these methods.

Resilience is intentional and deliberate thoughts, beliefs, and behaviors that keep you focused on your goal.

Journaling

Taking ten minutes at the start of your day can be special time you spend with yourself. This practice will open you up to parts of yourself that you otherwise would not have the chance to explore. The relief of tension is very quick as you write out what you have been holding onto inside. This practice can help you achieve the flow state and will build on your ability to stay in the moment.

There are many types of Journals. I suggest a few here and provide tips for this power tool and stress strategy.

Tips for Journaling

1. Give yourself the space to be distraction-free. Turn off your phone, social media, and anything else that will interrupt you.

2. Start this session of with a few deeps breaths on a count of four, and inhale some essential oils. Citrus blends are uplifting, peppermint is stimulating, and lavender is relaxing.

3. You can use the computer and type or handwrite in a journal. Many prefer writing it out and find this allows for greater flow.

4. Be sure to date your entries.

5. Begin to write (or type), and do not censor or edit. Just write for five minutes. Then, read what you have written. Ask yourself, "What does this mean for me?" and further explore what you have written.

6. Keep your journal private.

7. Journaling can be especially powerful after difficult *or* happy times. You can also set up a weekly ritual to write.

Types of Journals

1. *Idea Journal*
   Carry a notebook with you and jot down any ideas you have for a book, poem, fashion design, or any other creative pursuit that interests you. This may be a thought you have to explore later.

2. *Work Journal*
   Keep a notebook in the breakroom of your job and have staff write down things they are grateful for, acts of kindness, and observations they have. This can be related to Six Sigma projects, special initiatives, or a

general practice. Review at a staff meeting or during a special meeting to discuss 'matters of the heart' or the "Breakroom Conversation."

3. *Memory Book*
   Start a journal for your child, niece, or even a friends' baby and periodically write down what is happening, adding pictures and memorabilia. Have entries on the child's birthday, your birthday, and other special dates. Give it to the child on his or her sixth, tenth, or sixteenth birthday.

4. *Couple or Family Journal*
   Keep a journal in the kitchen and use this to communicate in happy times and especially with conflict. This can be used to focus on gratitude, family values, and also reflect on the growth years.

The BS of Stress: Your Belief System

What you believe drives your behavior. Stress changes your perception and can set up a skewed reaction to what is happening around you. This next process will reframe "stressed-out" reactions and highlight beliefs that may be sabotaging you, giving you the opportunity to do it differently next time.

This exercise is a very interesting way to shift your perception, attitudes, and behavior using a logical analysis of what happened. Strong emotions and compulsive thought loops can come from chronic stress, resulting in "stinkin' thinkin'"! This process we are going to review was developed by Albert Ellis, PhD, the father of Rational Emotive Behavior Therapy.

Hind sight is 20/20. Why? When you look back at the scenario that set you off, it is easier to be objective. This next process empowers you to recognize how your belief system fuels "stressed-out" reactions. You will learn how to do it differently, whereby interrupting destructive reactions.

These beliefs are your self-talk: your continuous, inner dialogue that is typically outside of the radar of your awareness. Yet, belief systems drive behavior, setting up consequences you may later regret. These beliefs get set up very early in life, and unless they are challenged, they permanently become part of your internal landscape and inner dialogue.

This exercise will help you quickly shift your perspective.

The ABC Process

A Activating event. Identify what precipitated your "stressed" reaction.

B Beliefs about the activating event. Beliefs may be evidenced immediately or may become more apparent

as you analyze the consequences.

C Consequences. What happened as a result of your "stressed" reaction?

D Dispute, debate, and differentiate as you analyze A, B, and C and discard what doesn't work.

E Evaluation. What happened as a result of the four Ds? What can you do differently next time?

Example

Earlier, you sent your boss an email about attending an upcoming workshop. Normally, she gets back to you right away. Several hours have passed, and you have not heard anything. You begin to feel fearful and angry that she has not responded to you, especially after all you have done for your department. You start thinking about all the times you stayed late to finish up projects, and the tension builds as you tell yourself how you are never appreciated. This all too familiar feeling turns to anger and resentment. At this point, you slam the door, and your coworkers start to worry that you are going to say something irrational. Before you send off another email to your boss about how she needs to spend more time on the frontline instead of in her safe cocoon of an office, you are interrupted by a coworker who lets you know your boss just arrived, having been delayed due to a huge accident on the beltway.

Slightly relieved, although embarrassed, you realize you wasted an hour getting upset over nothing and looking out of control to your team.

Activating Event: No response to your request to attend the workshop. Responses "usually" come quickly.

Beliefs: "I am not appreciated and do not get what I need." These are old inner thoughts going back to childhood stemming from never receiving appreciation from a parent who was preoccupied.

Consequence: Anger outburst, muttering under your breath, slamming the door, and appearing out of control to your team members.

Dispute: Objectively reviewing what happened; not getting an email is not a response. Clarify, get more information, and investigate *before* assuming the answer.

Evaluation: Getting all the facts is the first thing to do before letting the emotional storm take over. Work on healing deep-rooted resentment and the source of the "familiar" negative feelings. Use Tapping Techniques to release emotional charge.

Use this chart to work through some of the reactions you would like to change. You may be thinking, "This is too much work," and you might not feel like taking the time to do the exercise. I say get a notebook, create the chart, and get going. It is well worth it!

Here is an example of starting with a **consequence** and then working back to see what happened:

Activating Event	Beliefs	Consequences	Dispute	Evaluation
		Feel sad, hopeless, hungry, and worried. I crave sweets.		

What may be a trigger for these feelings?

Activating Event	Beliefs	Consequences	Dispute	Evaluation
Seeing my ex and not having a date for the party.		Feel sad, hopeless, hungry, and worried. I crave sweets.		

The key aspect of this exercise is to identify the **BS**—your *belief system* responsible for setting up the chain reaction. Tune in to your self-talk.

Activating Event	Beliefs	Consequences	Dispute	Evaluation
Seeing my ex and not having a date for the party.	*I can never trust men again. I don't need a date. I don't need anyone.*	Feel sad, hopeless, hungry, and worried. I crave sweets.		

This part of the exercise is meant to dispute your beliefs and discard those that are no longer true. Rigorously debate every aspect of your self-talk.

Activating Event	Beliefs	Consequences	Dispute	Evaluation
Seeing my ex and not having a date for the party.	I can never trust men again. I don't need a date. I don't need anyone.	Feel sad, hopeless, hungry, and worried. I crave sweets.	*1. One man is not all men. I can trust men. 2. I do not need a date, and I want to have fun and date. 3. I do need people in my life.*	

1. Where is the proof of your belief? List the factual evidence in support of your belief. Emotional storms may capture all of your attention and "feel" real. However, feelings are not facts.

2. List the "logical" explanations to explain the activating event. In the case of this example, seeing the ex and not having a date for the party were paired together as if one caused the other. They are two separate events. Your ex may make you feel like you can never get a date, but they are not really related.

3. If you were to give advice to someone about this event, what would you tell them? This forces you to be objective.

4. Have you been in a similar situation before only to find out that it was also a skewed perception? If you are prone to "awfulize," dramatize, or "catastrophize," you may have a pattern that is worth breaking up.

5. What have you learned from previous situations?

In the final phase of this process, complete the **Evaluation** column and write out how the process of debating and disputing **A**, **B**, and **C** shifted your perception or attitude.

This process is empowering and helps break through the **BS**— your **belief systems** that have had you stuck or derailed. Now, let's move on to another tool to break through the BS.

Turning Down the Heat: Irrational Beliefs

As you tune into your self-talk, do you "should" yourself? Is your inner dialogue filled with *musts*, *shoulds*, obligations, the word "no," *can'ts*, and other limiting words? The urgency that gets created with absolutes also increases the emotional charge that becomes a part of communication personally and professionally. The quality of the interaction within yourself and with others is foundational for strong emotional intelligence. These exercises will build your self-awareness and give you an opportunity to shift your behavior.

Have you ever gotten into a "heated" discussion? We all have been there and may, at times, have been the one to stoke the fire. There are certain words or phrases that create more heat in a conversation or team meeting than others.

For example, rage is a strong emotion that usually has dire consequences. Being irritated, annoyed, and frustrated are more manageable responses and at least allow for progress in the conversation. The more you tune in, the greater you can manage and tamp down the strong feelings for the wellbeing of the group or your goals.

Look out for self-talk like this:

- ✘ "This is awful."

- ✘ "I can't stand it!"

- ✘ "I am worthless."

- ✘ "Always," "should," and "never."

Use the previous exercise to work backward from this "consequence" and get to the **BS**—your **belief system** that started it.

The Power of Visualization: Staying Motivated

It is common and typical for motivation to wax and wane. You have probably experienced this when you have started a new diet or exercise plan or when you decided to change a bad habit. As daily life bears down and you get bogged down in the details of work and the demands of life, your goals for starting your new program may be further away in your mind and harder to get excited about.

It is important to remember the "why" of what you are doing and imagine the changes you want as a result of the change. In the beginning, motivation is at a high and everything is easy. As the weeks move on, your desires may seem less important as stress takes its toll on your enthusiasm. As challenges show up, your resolve to continue to adopt new behaviors may weaken.

You need a "motivation reboot."

What do you want to have happen? What will your day or life look like?

Define it, and then imagine it. Experience it, feel it, and get as detailed as possible. Hold the expectation. Really feel the achievement of this goal. Use this tool with all things big and small. Do you have trouble communicating with an employee? See your next conversation flowing smoothly. Do the same with your spouse, children, and friends. Release the struggle of trying too hard, and use visualization to see what you want to happen.

Worry is the negative use of visualization as people go over and over a scenario in their minds, increasing tension and confusion. It is important to stop the worry and use your imagination for your highest good.

Do you want new skills in communication, optimism, resilience, and emotional intelligence? See yourself interacting and succeeding. You do not have to figure out how this is going to happen. You are simply imagining what you want and, in essence, practicing the outcome! This is what athletes, musicians, and all successful people do. This is the competitive edge you will have as you adopt this power tool.

As life demands more of you, it is easy to give your energy to the urgency right in front of you, leaving yourself frustrated and feeling negative about what is possible. A regular habit of visualization will keep you focused on your goals.

Your motivation reboot means using your mind in its highest and best form. Your brain naturally uses images to communicate at all levels of your conscious and unconscious mind, and this is a quick way to reset focus without hard work.

Look, imagine, and believe.

Mindfulness

There is time enough for everything in the course of the day, if you do but one thing at once, but there is not time enough in the year if you will do two things at a time.
—Lord Chesterfield

Distraction is the New Normal

Do you keep your phone next to you and constantly check for texts, emails, Facebook posts, twitter, Instagram, and more?

Do you lose yourself on the internet and in social media?

Do you start reading and then realize by the end of the page you do not remember a single word?

Is it hard to focus and finish?

In the 90s, there was an excitement and pride in the ability to multitask. Cell phones were on the horizon, and there was a belief that one could do multiple things at once and do them well. Today, we know differently. We have fatalities that result from multitasking while driving, and 70% of the workforce is disengaged, costing billions.

Mindfulness Is a Form of Meditation

Mindfulness means directing your attention to what is happening in the moment. As you tune in, you are observing your experience rather than reacting to it. This means you simply notice what you are experiencing without trying to change what you are experiencing.

Let's look at an example. If you are hungry, most people are going to go search for something to eat. When many people feel anxious, tired, angry, or hurt they also go in search for something to eat. Before long, just about any feeling can be associated with hunger, and food becomes the universal solution.

So, how do you know if you are hungry or feeling an emotion?

Tuning into what you are feeling requires you first quiet your mind and break free of the distractions. This ability to focus inward relaxes your mind and body and increases your effectiveness.

As you go through your busy day wrapped up thoughts and feelings without a break, you may find it useful to check in. Stop and ask yourself, "What is happening right now, in this moment?"

As you get started, set your timer during the day to remind you to stop and tune in. What is going on within you? What do you feel?

Power Tip

Practice heart-focused breathing for three minutes. Now, what do you notice?

Mindful Eating

With lives that are on the go, fast food has become the norm. Over 75% of food that is eaten is processed and already prepared. This is only part of the problem; this food is eaten in a car, in front of the TV or computer, or while reading. You can double your caloric intake when you eat this way, as your body does not register what you have eaten.

Mindfulness Exercise

Next time you eat (and it doesn't matter what you eat), start by taking a few deep breaths, in on a count of four, hold on a count of four and then out on a count of four. Then, continue to breathe for about ten seconds. This should quiet your mind and help you focus on your food.

Think about all of the people and activity required to bring you this food. From the time the seeds were planted to all the processing that is required, transportation, and your own effort in preparation. Stay with this imagery as you experience gratitude and appreciation for this effort. Breathe regularly and easily as you imagine this.

Now, look at the food. Take in the colors, smells, and texture. Chew each bite and notice what is happening in your mouth as you chew. Just focus on your experience as you eat. It is normal for your mind to wander as you start this practice; simply notice and then bring it back to your food.

Eating slower and very tuned in to yourself, you will recognize when you feel satisfied. Stop eating before you feel full. Your stomach digests best when it is two-thirds full. Stop eating. Wrap up the rest of your food and push away from the table. Take a few sips of water to refresh your palette, and breathe deep for ten seconds.

Mindfulness is an exercise you can practice at any time. Use your breath to bring you back to a quiet place so you can keep your attention on what is going on in the moment. Keep a journal handy as you may find yourself gaining insights into your choices and behavior.

On a Count of Four, Breathe!

This is a very simple practice that will yield powerful results. You are breathing anyway; this is just breathing with intention and the goal to shift the stress effect.

The majority of people today are in moderate to severe stress, multitasking, or in the throes of strong emotions. Breathing gets shallow and less effective in blowing off the buildup of CO_2, leaving you more acidic—the opposite of what the body needs to be to stay energized. This shallow way of breathing becomes a habit.

Start by taking four deep breaths: in on the count of four, hold on a count of four and exhaling on the count of four. Breathe in through your nose and out your mouth.

Now, think about something for which you are grateful, like the short line at the gas pump or the recent promotion, your health, your grandchildren, your pet, or your job—anything that helps you experience the feeling of gratitude.

Continue this for 20 seconds, longer if possible. Just bring yourself back to the feelings of gratitude and release any thoughts. Do this two to three times a day. This produces long-term results. This actually builds your resilience, increasing your capacity for stress and improving your wellbeing.

Rapid Release Methods: Tapping Techniques

Tapping is one of the many techniques in Energy Psychology that "work" by clearing the energy field. Chinese medicine uses a meridian system with different acupressure and acupuncture techniques to optimize the flow of the life force, the *chi*. Traditional medicine, at this point, only recognizes the energy field in diagnostics (MRI, CAT scan) and does not engage this field for any type of treatment—yet. This simple tapping technique is very effective in releasing anxiety, fears, phobias, anger, and negativity. I have included it among the Stress Strategies as I have used this with thousands of people in a variety of circumstances and have seen it work dramatically.

There are videos and research on it as part of the online Resilient Leader program.

This energy field can become blocked and or stagnant as a result of diet, toxins, traumas, and strong emotions as in chronic stress. Not drinking enough water is enough to interrupt the flow of your life force energy. As your energy field becomes blocked and weakened, you are at risk for many health challenges along with problems with focus, mood, concentration, and energy. Chinese medicine recognizes energy channels that move the life force, or *chi*, throughout your mind, body, and spirit.

Tapping techniques (TT) use simple

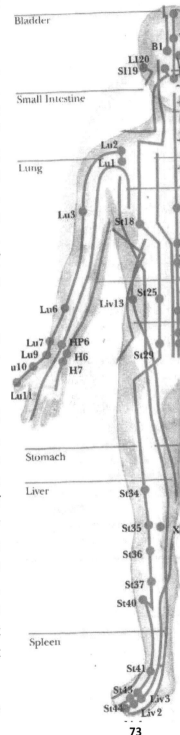

acupressure on points on the face and hands to release this blocked energy that can show up as fears, phobias, anxiety, negativity, headaches, tension, and so much more. Tapping has been found to work effectively on pain, nausea, and many other "physical" problems as well. Tapping is a good tool to balance your energy field for greater performance and more joy.

Tapping techniques are so simple and easy to use—we suggest you try it on everything! More than 85% of the time, it works within five minutes!

Wouldn't you like to feel more calm and centered? Many people discount the results because they don't understand *how* this could possibly work. When you turn on the lights, do you really have to know *how* this energy is moving through the wires before you flip the switch? So it is with TT. When you tap, you may not know exactly how it works, but if you get results in five to fifteen minutes a day, does it really matter?

What you believe sets up expectations. If you think only of the worst case scenarios, then that is what you condition yourself to expect. TT will clear your negative and limiting beliefs and the emotional overtones that support those beliefs.

What do you spend your time predicting about your life? Which thoughts keep you stuck?

Your belief system will activate your potential *or* hold you back. Your thoughts, beliefs, and emotions either support optimal health and success, or they set you up for failure and even physical disease.

What you focus on grows, so if you live in fear, then you create fear experiences. You always have a choice about what kind of movie to play in your mind as you go about your day. However, there are times when you may feel stuck or unable to change this movie. Becoming more aware of what you say to yourself or the emotional pattern with which you live is key to releasing these blocks. By using this simple, rapid release tool, you can shift out of the negativity into a positive and empowered mindset.

We provide audio and video in the online program that takes you through the tapping sequence. Tapping is very effective in releasing limiting beliefs and blocks to greater joy and peace. TT is simple and will work even if you do not believe it will. You just have to use it.

We hope you use this simple tapping technique whenever you feel anything that is distressing. Use it as you think about the argument with your partner or coworker or friend.

Tap as you drive home from work to release any fallout from your day.

Tap before you go to bed at night to release any leftover attachments to your day.

Use it on your children as they talk about their day to help them release any distressing feelings. Tap along with them, and you will also release any stressful feelings.

How to Tap

Study the diagram on the next page (*Fig. 3*). Here is the step-by-step process for the acupressure technique:

1. Identify your fear, difficult emotion, or stressful feeling. Be as specific as you can. Note your level of distress before you begin tapping and after. Measure the

emotional charge associated with the issue you chose to tap on using a scale of one to ten (ten being the worst).

2. After identifying the fear, difficult emotion, or thought, find your "sore spot" on your *left* chest area while rubbing it firmly and repeating this three times: "Even though I have 'this problem,' I deeply and completely accept myself..."

3. Then, begin tapping at the edge of the eyebrow and follow the complete sequence of points on one side. While you tap, think about the stressful event, difficult conversation, or feelings that are troubling you. You can talk or stay silent; just focus on the negative feelings. This will release the intensity and help you shift out of the negative to a more relaxed and neutral place.

4. Continue tapping this sequence of points for three to four rounds, going through all the points. Stop, take a deep breath, and tune into the emotional charge. How would you rate it now? Continue to tap until your distress reaches zero to one.

5. You may need to repeat this sequence a number of times. Persistence does pay off. You may have other emotions surface as the one you started with fades. Tune in to what you are feeling, and if it is different, make note so you can tap on that later. Stay focused on your original issue until it rates zero to one. Then, go to the other issues that come up.

Once cleared, the problem does not usually come up again. The memory of the problem remains, but the emotional charges are gone.

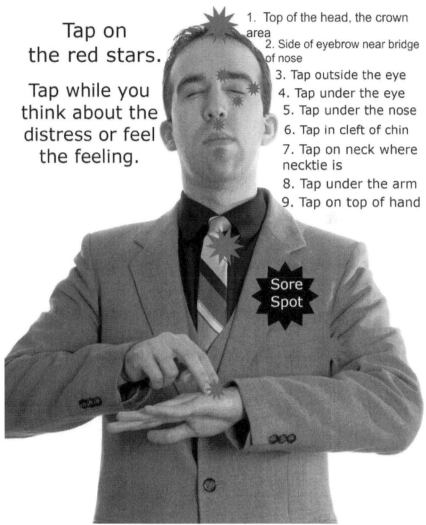

Tap on
the red stars.

Tap while you
think about the
distress or feel
the feeling.

1. Top of the head, the crown area
2. Side of eyebrow near bridge of nose
3. Tap outside the eye
4. Tap under the eye
5. Tap under the nose
6. Tap in cleft of chin
7. Tap on neck where necktie is
8. Tap under the arm
9. Tap on top of hand

Sore
Spot

Fig. 2

Aromatherapy

Using therapeutic-grade essential oils is a great strategy to calm, focus, and balance your nervous system as well as boost your immune system. This is important because with chronic stress, your immune system is weakened.

Bergamot, citrus oils, and lavender are good choices to uplift and calm your spirit. Essential oils are the life blood of the plant, and they have many powerful uses and benefits.

Whether it is to support emotional wellbeing, digestion, or the immune system, essential oils are nature's pharmacy.

Integrating the use of therapeutic-grade essential oils for overall health and wellbeing is an ancient practice that continues to have great benefits today. In this brief introduction to the use of therapeutic essential oils, we will discuss using oils for comfort and relaxation for yourself as well as with your family.

A Few Facts about Essential Oils

- EOs enhance the body's natural ability to balance and restore itself.
- EOs act as a catalyst to encourage blood cells to deliver and carry more oxygen and nutrients to encourage regeneration and natural detoxification.
- EOs make oxygen more available in the body as opposed to oxidizing and generating free radicals.
- EOs enhance the "energy field" and boost the immune system.

- EOs are antibacterial, anti-viral, and anti-fungal, anti-parasitic, and antiseptic.
- EOs are adaptogenic, working on the need most present and balancing mind, body, and spirit.
- EOs are absorbed and go to work in the body in a matter of *seconds*.

Olfaction and the Brain

Research in olfactory perception has shown that it only takes exposure to a few molecules to have a significant effect on you. The smell of chocolate chip cookies or freshly mowed grass can instantly recreate memories and bring up past associations. Smell has an effect on your central nervous system. Fragrance researchers are discovering that odors can and do influence mood, evoke emotions, counteract stress, and even reduce high blood pressure.

It has only been in the last twenty years that research into the olfactory system (*Fig. 4*) has begun to reveal the mysteries of

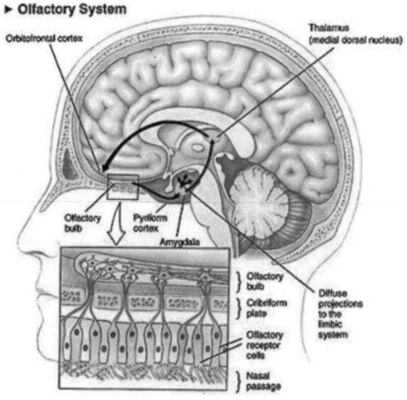

Fig. 4

how aromas are processed and interpreted by the body.

The sense of smell is highly developed in animals and is important to detect food, identify enemies, mark territory, and identify the opposite sex. This sense of smell is a form of communication.

In humans, the sense of smell is highly sophisticated. However, it is not relied on for survival, except when the smell of gas, smoke, or decaying food alerts one to danger.

Smell is actually important in flavor perception; much of what you might taste is actually smell. In a research study where smell was inhibited, things like coffee and chocolate—which are identified over 90% of the time—were not correctly identified by any of the subjects! Our sense of smell is more sensitive than any other part of the nervous system. We can discriminate over 10,000 different odors with many odors having only minor differences. Most common smells represent a mixture of odors.

Smell is the only sense in which the receptor nerve endings are in direct contact with the outside world. The olfactory bulb does not require the cortex to process the information. Olfactory nerve cells are also the only nerve cells that repair themselves if damaged.

Smell begins in the nasal cavity and proceeds to the olfactory bulb where "messages" are initially processed. Then, it is off to the higher centers of the olfactory system where perception and memory is triggered. The second target is the limbic system where emotions and behaviors are triggered. Because of the proximity to the hypothalamus, essential oils may also influence hormonal response. Together with the limbic system, the hypothalamus governs primitive drives—thirst, sex, hunger—while also invoking gut feeling reactions such as fear, rage, sadness, attraction, and affection.

Final Words

Congratulations! If you have read this entire book, you are on your way to a renewed sense of purpose in your life. I look forward to seeing you at the retreat and in the Mastermind Program. To become an authentic and resilient leader, you need ongoing support and a commitment to eliminate the risks of losing momentum.

How will you put these suggestions into practice? How will you continue to look within and develop those skills that will make you effective and dynamic as a leader? There is so much competing for our attention today, and you must choose how to spend your time and resources.

The Resilient Leader System is an investment in yourself, your future, and opportunities never before possible for you. I can say this because I have seen this consistently with my clients—

they go on to achieve success far beyond what they initially thought possible.

This can happen for you as well. Believe in yourself. I do.

Please let me know how these strategies have worked for you.

Visit my Facebook page, Vibrant Radiant Health. I will be holding monthly Q & A and webinars and this is a great way to stay in touch.

You can also sign up for my weekly newsletter at www.vibrantradianthealth.com

Please share your thoughts, experiences and questions about this book.

I look forward to meeting you soon!

Appendix

Self-Assessment: Five-Dimension Evaluation of Wellbeing

This simple self-assessment helps you tune into these five ways you can support your wellbeing on a daily basis. Evaluate yourself and answer based on the one (low) to ten (high) scale. Think about your life overall, and average your responses.

To score each section, add up the numbers given to each question and divide by 10.

Relationships (Connection)

Wellbeing is enhanced when relationships are nurtured. This requires your time and attention.

1. I make time to spend with my family. 1 2 3 4 5 6 7 8 9 10

2. I am happy with the amount of time spent with friends. 1 2 3 4 5 6 7 8 9 10

3. I make time for my partner every day. 1 2 3 4 5 6 7 8 9 10

4. I make time to talk with my children about what is happening in their lives. 1 2 3 4 5 6 7 8 9 10

5. I make the time to get to know my co-workers and/or my staff. 1 2 3 4 5 6 7 8 9 10

6. I like myself and am comfortable with who I am. 1 2 3 4 5 6 7 8 9 10

7. I am satisfied with my closest relationships. 1 2 3 4 5 6 7 8 9 10

8. I have fun in my personal relationships. 1 2 3 4 5 6 7 8 9 10

9. I am productive in my work relationships. 1 2 3 4 5 6 7 8 9 10

10. My relationships are balanced in give and take. 1 2 3 4 5 6 7 8 9 10

TOTAL _____ ÷ 10 = _____

How can you improve your relationships?

Energy and Vibrant Health

Wellbeing requires you to have energy physically, emotionally, and spiritually. Your everyday choices and lifestyle make the difference in how much energy you have.

1. I exercise at least twenty minutes four out of seven days.   1 2 3 4 5 6 7 8 9 10

2. I eat vegetables and fruit daily; minimum of 3 servings.   1 2 3 4 5 6 7 8 9 10

3. I drink at least eight eight-ounce glasses of water each day.   1 2 3 4 5 6 7 8 9 10

4. For every fast food meal eaten in a week, subtract a point from the total of ten (i.e., 1x, 2x, 3x a day X days of the week).   1 2 3 4 5 6 7 8 9 10

5. I wake up feeling rested.   1 2 3 4 5 6 7 8 9 10

6. I drink coffee or energy drinks to get going. Subtract a point for every drink to boost energy in the week.   1 2 3 4 5 6 7 8 9 10

7. I am satisfied with my weight.   1 2 3 4 5 6 7 8 9 10

8. I have maintained my weight in the last month.   1 2 3 4 5 6 7 8 9 10

9. I have all the energy I need to do what I have to do in the day.   1 2 3 4 5 6 7 8 9 10

10. I have the energy to be creative.   1 2 3 4 5 6 7 8 9 10

TOTAL _____ ÷ 10 = _____

What can you change or add that will have the most impact on your energy?

Meaning/Purpose (Give Back)

People who experience the highest levels of wellbeing have found ways to engage in meaningful activities. This could be at work, hobbies, or in support of various causes. The ability to live life knowing you are expressing your purpose is an important aspect of wellbeing.

1. I engage in a daily spiritual practice with prayer, meditation, and mindfulness.   1 2 3 4 5 6 7 8 9 10

2. I am guided by core values in my daily life.   1 2 3 4 5 6 7 8 9 10

3. I make choices based on my values.   1 2 3 4 5 6 7 8 9 10

4. I feel fulfilled.   1 2 3 4 5 6 7 8 9 10

5. I volunteer my time.   1 2 3 4 5 6 7 8 9 10

6. I support causes important to me with time or money.   1 2 3 4 5 6 7 8 9 10

7. I "unplug" every four hours for at least fifteen minutes.   1 2 3 4 5 6 7 8 9 10

8. I enjoy quiet time in nature.   1 2 3 4 5 6 7 8 9 10

9. I spend time alone and reflect on my life and accomplishments.   1 2 3 4 5 6 7 8 9 10

10. I am inspired by the miracles that show up in my life.   1 2 3 4 5 6 7 8 9 10

TOTAL _____ ÷ 10 = _____

What can you do to bring more meaning into your life?

Resilience (Keep Going)

Being able to adapt and keep going is the difference between success and failure. Life happens, and while you cannot control the events, you can control how you respond.

1. I have all the time I need in a day.   1   2   3   4   5   6   7   8   9   1 0

2. I see the glass half-full.   1   2   3   4   5   6   7   8   9   1 0

3. I am in charge of my personal life.   1   2   3   4   5   6   7   8   9   1 0

4. I am in charge of my professional life.   1   2   3   4   5   6   7   8   9   1 0

5. I easily adapt to the daily challenges that show up.   1   2   3   4   5   6   7   8   9   1 0

6. I manage stress well.   1   2   3   4   5   6   7   8   9   1 0

7. I balance the demands in my day and also give myself time.   1   2   3   4   5   6   7   8   9   1 0

8. I bounce back from setbacks.   1   2   3   4   5   6   7   8   9   1 0

9. I acknowledge mistakes and/or failures and keep going.   1   2   3   4   5   6   7   8   9   1 0

10. I show up every day and do the best I can.   1   2   3   4   5   6   7   8   9   1 0

TOTAL _____ ÷ **10 =** _____

Do you need to adjust your attitude? In what way?

Growth (Self-Care)

Taking care of yourself may be one of the hardest things to do and the most important. It is the foundation of wellbeing.

1. I take care of myself first and then take care of others. 1 2 3 4 5 6 7 8 9 10

2. I receive as much as I give in my personal relationships. 1 2 3 4 5 6 7 8 9 10

3. I make time for my needs. 1 2 3 4 5 6 7 8 9 10

4. I can say no without feeling guilty. 1 2 3 4 5 6 7 8 9 10

5. I spend money on personal development. 1 2 3 4 5 6 7 8 9 10

6. I think about what I need throughout the day. 1 2 3 4 5 6 7 8 9 10

7. I build in time for hobbies every week. 1 2 3 4 5 6 7 8 9 10

8. I am aware of when I need "me" time. 1 2 3 4 5 6 7 8 9 10

9. I easily communicate my needs to others and respect their needs. 1 2 3 4 5 6 7 8 9 10

10. I look at myself in the mirror and enjoy what I see. 1 2 3 4 5 6 7 8 9 10

TOTAL _____ **÷ 10 =** _____

What can you do every day to grow?

Resilience Map

Use this spider graph to plot your scores from each section. You can easily see how balanced you are and what areas can use extra attention.

Plot your scores from each dimension of wellbeing

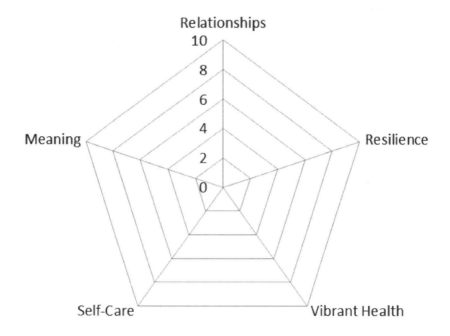

Three Things I Will Do More of to Increase Balance and Wellbeing	Three Things I Will Do Less of to Increase Balance and Wellbeing
1.	1.
2.	2.
3.	3.

Five Ways to Wellbeing in Practice

1. Imagine yourself starting the day by tuning in to yourself and setting your intention. **(Connect.)**
   I intend today to be successful.

2. Drink a glass of water with fresh lemon instead of coffee. Practice heart-focused breathing for three minutes. **(Energize.)**
3. Smile more at people you see on the street or in your office. **(Give.)**
4. Spend your lunch in a mindfulness state of mind as you eat. **(Grow.)**
5. Regardless of the events, keep a positive attitude. **(Keep Going.)**

Accelerate Your Performance with the Resilient Leader System

The RLS helps you consistently perform at a higher level for greater satisfaction and fulfillment on and off the job.

The program consists of one-on-one coaching, retreats, and a Mastermind Program. This process includes the leading

assessment for emotional intelligence, EQi 2.0, giving you a baseline of your strengths and an action plan for further development.

Included in the program is a 100-page workbook divided into two sections: Leading Yourself and Leading Others. This gives you suggestions and exercises to help you hold yourself and your team accountable.

You will have access to an online program with audio and video on the dimensions of EI and skills that are part of high-performance leadership.

The goal of the program is greater satisfaction, confidence, mental focus, and flexibility.

Here is what one participant has said:

"This program changed my life. I have concrete tools I can use with my team and I have finally learned to honor my strengths. This confidence takes the struggle out of my day since I no longer have to second guess myself."

—Danielle F., DNP, Director of Emergency Services

Contact us today and schedule a complimentary Power-Up Session to see what the Resilient Leader System can do for you.

Toll-free: 1-866-300-6360

www.resilientleaderprogram.com

Coaching is the single greatest accelerator for change.

The Resilient Leader VIP Retreat

One-Day Workshop Conducted by Dr. Cynthia

Now you and your leadership team can learn the most important strategies and be revitalized in this retreat format.

This dynamic one-day program includes:

- ✓ A leadership assessment prior to the retreat providing a baseline emotional intelligence assessment.
- ✓ Your own Action Plan to focus your effort.
- ✓ 100-page workbook, ten competency card decks on EI, and a Success Journal.
- ✓ Access to online audio and videos.
- ✓ Introduction to the dimensions of EI that will develop your consistent high performance.
- ✓ Introduction to five-minute strategies to unhook you from the stress reaction.
- ✓ A proven system that will ensure you achieve the balance you need to work SMART.

www.vipleadershipretreat.com

The Resilient Leader Mastermind Program

Ongoing Group Program with Dr. Cynthia via the Phone/Web

Ever wish you had access to other like-minded leaders focused on success?

Tired of feeling alone in your leadership role?

What if you could have support, resources, professional coaching, and facilitation so you could grow, learn, and develop an even greater ability to persuade, influence, and motivate your people?

The Mastermind Program is a historic format that moves people quickly into high performance by keeping up your momentum and desire to achieve while holding you accountable. This small group program gives you time to work on specific challenges while learning from others in the group.

www.successthroughmastermind.com

About the Author

Cynthia Howard RN, CNC, PhD is the leading High-Performance Coach for professionals, leaders, and executives in healthcare.

Cynthia is a mentor, coach, and resilience champion, and in the past twenty-plus years, she has coached thousands of individuals to consistently perform at a high level for greater success and fulfillment.

Dr. Cynthia integrates the latest research in the fields of flow, resilience, emotional intelligence, and high performance with her experience in energy management. This combination offers rapid, lasting change.

To contact Cynthia about this program, speaking at your organization, or how this program can transform your leadership, call toll-free at 1-866-300-6360 or email drh@vibrantradianthealth.com.

www.vibrantradianthealth.com

Live from your core. Being authentic is how
you connect with your power.

The world needs leaders who have the courage to take risks.

Recommended Resources

American Nurses Credentialing Center. (2006). "Benefits of becoming a magnet-designated facility." <http://www.nursingworld.org/ancc/magnet/benes.html>.

Bass, B. M. (1985). *Leadership and Performance*. New York, NY: Free Press.

Burns, J. M. (1978). *Leadership*. New York, NY: Harper and Row.

Barrios-Choplin, Bob, PhD, McCraty, Rollin, Ph.D., Sundram, Joseph, M.Ed. and Atkinson, Mike. (1999). "The Effect of Employee Self-Management Training on Personal and Organizational Quality." HeartMath Research Center, Institute of HeartMath. Publication No. 99-083. Boulder Creek, CA.

Barrios-Choplin, Bob, PhD, McCraty, Rollin, Ph.D. ,Cryer, Bruce, MA. (1997). "An inner quality approach to reducing stress and improving physical and emotional well-being at work." *Stress Medicine*. Vol 13.193-201.

EQi 2.0 Workplace Report. (2011). Multi Health Systems.

Erickson, R., & Grove, W. (2007, October). "Why emotions matter: Age, agitation, and burnout among registered nurses." *Online Journal of Issues in Nursing*. 13(1).

Fromm, Erich (1956). *The Art of Loving*. Harper and Row.

Holt, Jim. "Time Bandits: What were Einstein and Gödel talking about?" *New Yorker*, February 28, 2005.

Howard, Cynthia (2012). "Use This Simple Tool to Transform Your Stress and Avoid Nursing Burnout. Part 1 and 2." *Nurse Together*. <http://www.nursetogether.com/Lifestyle/Life style-Article>.

Silow-Carroll, Sharon, Alteras, Tanya, & Meyer, Jack A. (2007, April). "Hospital quality improvement: Strategies and lessons from U.S. hospitals." *Health Management Associates.*

Stein, Steven J., & Book, Howard E. *The EQ edge: Emotional intelligence and your success.* Ontario, Canada: Jossey Bass. 211.

Sy T., Cote S., Saavedra R. (2005). "The Contagious Leader: Impact of the Leader's Mood on the Mood of Group Members, Group Affective Tone, and Group Processes." *Journal of Applied Psychology*, 2005. Vol. 90, No. 2, 295–305.

Thompson, Henry. (2010). *The Stress Effect.* San Francisco, CA: Jossey Bass

Endnotes

[1] Aiken, Linda H., PhD, RN; Clarke, Sean P., PhD, RN; Sloane, Douglas M., PhD; Sochalski, Julie, PhD, RN, & Silber, Jeffrey H., MD, PhD. (2002, October). "Nurse staffing and patient mortality, nurse burnout, and job dissatisfaction." JAMA, 23/30, 288(16): 1987-1993.

[2] Price Waterhouse Cooper's Health Research Institute. (2007). "What works: Healing the healthcare staffing shortage." <http://pwchealth.com/cgi-local/hregister.cgi/reg/pubwhatworks.pdf>.

[3] Salt, J., Cummings, G.G., & Profetto-McGrath, J. (2008, June). "Increasing retention of new graduate nurses: A systematic review of interventions by healthcare organizations." *J Nurs Adm.* 38(6), 287-296.

[4] Howard, Cynthia. (1998). Archetypal emanations: A phenomenological inquiry into experienced nurses journeys through hospital restructuring. College Park, MD: University of Maryland Press.

[5] Stone, Robyn I., with Wiener, Joshua M. (2001, May). Who will care for us? Addressing the long-term care workforce crisis. The Urban Institute. <http://aspe.hhs.gov/daltcp/reports/ltcwf.htm>.

[6] Branham, Leigh. (2005). *7 Hidden Reason Employees Leave.* New York, NY: Amacom.

[7] Needleman, Jack, Ph.D., Buerhaus, Peter, Ph.D., RN, Pankratz, V. Shane, Ph.D., Leibson, Cynthia L., Ph.D., Stevens, Susanna R., M.S., & Harris, Marcelline, Ph.D., RN. (2011). "Nurse staffing and inpatient hospital mortality." *New England Journal of Medicine, 364,* 1037-1045.

[8] Buerhaus, Peter I., Auerbach, David I., & Staiger, Douglas O. (2009) "The Recent Surge in Nurse Employment: Causes and Implications." Health Affairs. July/August 2009 vol. 28 no. 4. 657-668.

[9] Bureau of Labor Statistics, Economic News Release. The Employment Summary, July 2012. <www.bls.gov/news.release/empsit.nr0.htm>.

See also Bureau of Labor Statistics, Economic News Release. Table 6. The 30 occupations with the largest projected employment growth, 2010-20. <http://www.bls.gov/news.release/ecopro.t06.htm>.

[10] American Association of Colleges of Nursing, Media Relations, Fact Sheet, Nursing Shortage. Updated August 6, 2012. <http://www.aacn.nche.edu/media-relations/fact-sheets/nursing-shortage>.

[11] Kaiser Family Foundation, the Agency for Healthcare Research and Quality, & the Harvard School of Public Health. (2004). *National Survey on Consumers' Experiences with Patient Safety and Quality Information.* <http://www.kff.org/kaiserpolls/ pomr111704pkg.cfm>.

[12] Cimiotti, Jeannie P., Aiken, Linda H., Sloane, Douglas M., & Wu, Evan S. "Nurse staffing, burnout, and health care–associated infection." *American Journal of Infection Control, August 2012, 40*(6), 486-490.

[13] Kovner, Christine T., PhD, RN, FAAN, Brewer, Carol S., PhD, RN, Fairchild, Susan, MPH, Poornima, Shakthi, MS, Kim, Hongsoo, PhD, RN, & Djukic, Maja, MS, RN. (2007, September). "Newly licensed RNs' characteristics, work attitudes, and intentions to work." American Journal of Nursing, 107 (9), 58–70.

[14] American Nurses Association, Health and Safety Survey, August 2011. <http://www. nursingworld.org/2011HealthSurveyResults.aspx>.

[15] Clifton, Jim. "High-Energy Workplaces Can Save America." *Business Journal*, December 14, 2011.

[16] Kleinman, Carol. (2004, Fall). "The relationship between managerial leadership behaviors and staff nurse retention." Hospital Topics: Research and Perspectives on Healthcare. 7 82 (4).

[17] Miller, Sally K., PhD, APN, FAANP, Alpert, Patricia T., DrPH, APN, FAANP, & Cross, Chad L., PhD, NCC, MAC, LADC. (2008, May). "Overweight and obesity in nurses, advanced practice nurses, and nurse educators." Journal of the American Academy of Nurse Practitioners, 20(5), 259–265.

18 May, Jessica H., Bazzoli, Gloria J., & Gerland, Anneliese M. (2006, July). "Hospitals' responses to nurse staffing shortages." Health Affairs. 25(4).

19 Branham, Leigh. (2005). *7 Hidden Reason Employees Leave*. New York, NY: Amacom.

20 Howard, Cynthia. (2015) *HEAL: Healthy Emotions. Abundant Life. A Toolkit to Master Your Life.* Santa Maria, CA: Vibrant Radiant Health

21 Goleman, Daniel. (1995). *Emotional intelligence: Why it matters more than IQ.* New York, NY: Bantam Dell.

22 Clance, P. R. (1985). *The Impostor Phenomenon: When Success Makes You Feel Like A Fake.* Toronto: Bantam Books.

See also Clance, Pauline Rose; Imes, Suzanne A. (1978). "The imposter phenomenon in high achieving women: Dynamics and therapeutic intervention." (PDF). *Psychotherapy: Theory, Research & Practice* 15 (3): 241–247.

23 Whitney, William Dwight, and Benjamin E. Smith. *The Century Dictionary and Cyclopedia.* New York: Century, 1901.

24 George, Bill. (2003). *Authentic Leadership: Rediscovering the Secrets to Creating Lasting Value.* San Francisco: Jossey-Bass.

25 Csikszentmihalyi, Mihaly. *Flow: The Psychology of Optimal Experience.* New York: Harper & Row, 1990. Print.